S0-BNT-834

4

Legendary

Dear Pam

Legendary

Jaiya John

To Praise and Cherish Your Kind Heart and Life!

SW🜚R

Soul Water Rising

Silver Spring, Maryland

4.28.11

Legendary

Copyright © 2008 by Jaiya John

All rights reserved under International and Pan-American Copyright Conventions.

No part of this book may be reproduced or transmitted in any form or by any means electronic or mechanical including photocopying, recording, or by any information storage and retrieval system, without permission in writing from the publisher, except by a reviewer, who may quote brief passages in a review. Address inquiries to fyi@soulwater.org.

Printed in the United States of America

Soul Water Rising
Silver Spring, Maryland
http://www.soulwater.org

Library of Congress Control Number: 2008908508
ISBN 978-0-9713308-4-9

FIRST SOUL WATER RISING EDITION: 2008

Poetry | Youth Social Services & Education

Editors:
Jacqueline V. Richmond
Kent W. Mortensen

Cover design: R. Eric Stone

Look at that young cat
singin' the blues
he's not complaining
just exclaiming:

my pain has a purpose
like splinters in the pews

I'm deeper cause
I've been to the deepness
my journey brings good news

now put down your troubles
and help me to sing these blues

"In the beginning were the instructions. We were to have compassion for one another, to live and work together, to depend on each other for support. We were told we were all related and interconnected to each other."

Tesuque Pueblo Elder

AUTHOR'S NOTE

She must have been only in her forties. Thick locks of hair falling over cavernous eyes. Those eyes. Pools of emotion overflowing their banks, dropping tears into the lagoon of my compassion. Leaning over the table, she took my hand and said to me in a determined voice, "Thank you for giving me the strength to carry on. You reminded me why I do this work. And why not everyone does. Honestly, I have felt burned out and weary. I was considering a change of careers. Thank you, just for understanding."

Such moments have occurred hundreds of times in brief intimate moments of honesty I have been blessed to share with people during my speaking engagements and in correspondence. A great majority of my audiences are teachers, social workers, counselors, advocates, mentors, and the like. So often they serve children and youth who have been devalued by a demanding society. A culture that assigns worth to our young based on social norms.

When our young do not meet those norms, they suffer the ransacking assault of daily derogation that pillages self-love from their very breast. These are youth who have committed the *offenses* of being materially impoverished; separated from family; homeless; or challenged in learning, behavior, mental health, or physical ability. Or they have *sinned* due to their heritage, language, or trauma from abuse or neglect. They are a collective aching heart and their numbers are massive.

This book, these poems and poetic stories, are for those who honorably serve our devalued young. They honor not because of their vocation, but because of the spirit in which they conduct their service. Their personal ethic will not let them betray the often hard truth of what must be done for a child. Their vision penetrates the sometimes illusory surface persona of youth to see the beauty and promise that live within. They summon the courage to reckon with their prejudices, shed their egos, and release their own greatness. A true teacher is in fact a social worker, given to the task of cultivating through children our collective social well-being. A true social worker is certainly a teacher, daring enough to enlighten both youth and colleague, according to not what is popular, but what is essential.

All who serve in this manner have earned the high title of being both teacher and social worker. They tend a sacred garden of youthfulness. We must elevate their name. They are underpaid and uncelebrated by our culture. We ask the world of them but provide slight and fickle support as they toil against youthful struggle in all its enormity. They are not celebrities, athletes, or tycoons. Yet their brave, enduring devotion truly lives on in the immeasurable ripple of goodness that feeds generations. My prayer is that such servants will drink from these words and be filled.

She speaks to her graduating class
of social work students
with a melancholy heart

for she has come to love them
they in their bright plumage of anticipation
clamoring for change

she knows that from the first moment
these missionaries step into human lives
they will be touched in ways profound

it is they who will be changed

her message is a tender plucking of strings
a spanish guitar ballad before eager dancers

a serenade:

Ours is a unique path
we are flagpoles for social justice
we acknowledge injustice

we insert social duty to the vulnerable
into a conversation enamored
with power and wealth

we advocate for change
empower the masses to address
the injustices heaped on their souls

we identify with the oppressed
this is not a mind game or trickery of association
we dig deep and discover that we *are* the oppressed
they are a physical extension of our own existence

we appear to stand as plants distinct from them
occupying different plots of the garden
yet ultimately our roots grow from the same ground
are nourished and poisoned by the same soil

we inhabit the same garden
breathe the same air

what ails the oppressed will reach us in time
our neglect of inequity returns to us magnified

identifying with indigent lives
is no cute condescension
it is the hard realization
that our physical body serves
as no boundary at all
when despair chooses to crawl

if we do not care for the least and distant
we endanger our most beloved

this world a flood plain
for all that we allow to be

we plant dignity and worth in the same ground
that arrogance plants its acid seed

where the world plants salt and lye
we plant richness and lime

human relations make the world barren
human relations can make barrenness a paradise

integrity is a hard coin to find
on the streets of hedonism
yet we search for its shine
in gutters and drains

holding fast to excellence
in flood tide of mediocrity

territorial temptations lead us
into phantom kingdoms where
we believe we rule the land

but in time our possessiveness
strangles the vines

we wake up cold and chilled in the night
to discover that we rule nothing but
dust mites and weeds

all souls desert a territory possessed

no place is worse than a troll-patrolled house
nothing grows in kingdoms ruled by a mouse

the modest serve greatly
the blowhards blow harder
but lose at the barter
between greatness and shame

downtrodden lose at the game
but their day too comes
when the tables have turned

and who was rich in pocket
but poor in the heart
finds all that was valued
has crumpled and burned

and all that was despised
has grown through the cries
to become rich in the soul
and favored by the skies

we who walk this road
must never stop learning

for the dark cloud of ignorance
never stops burning

and we must be faithful
for how can we teach our children to hope
unless we believe that change
is ever a possible and ordained thing

history looks favorably on she
who gives her life to humanity

its scrolls carry the tale of honorable
servants with the gift of many tongues

able to speak and decipher
the myriad languages of
suffering and promise

children howl in a special code
citizens react as if knowing what
they are trying to communicate

yet they have not bothered
to decipher the neophyte language

but we have

and we must be honest
for comfortable lives often build
fortresses constructed of lies

but pain blisters the paint on such walls
leaving the broken homeless indeed

only honesty builds character
that passes the muster

so walk through the veil of pain
bless yourself with all it reveals
your purpose lies beyond the veil

my students
we must be role models of compassion
for the world's faculty is fat with instructors
who write cold lesson plans

do not look for leadership into a better world
become that leadership

move the world.

9.6.08

The coach and the preacher
meet with the teacher
together they draft a declaration:

What happens to a school house
whose souls have been stolen?

what of the teeters that don't totter
the swings lonesome for bottoms to bear?

the playground once so fancy
now strident and *safe*
its grass gone to dust?

 we don't mean to make a fuss
and yet we must   we must

we hear no squeaking of shoes
on the gym floor as we used to

administration exclaims the high liability
of children who run

what of their bodies that never see sun?
what of their bellies swollen on sugar
their arteries gathering their plaque

by age 40 the coming of their
non-liable heart attack?

the hallways are dreary
which should not surprise us
after all music was banished so long ago

just after colors were bleached from bleachers
and up went the barbed wire fences and walls

we have to teach them the basics
or we'll fail them   they say

what of the failure of joy
given no time to play?

what of the clouds children
used to daydream about?

what of their doodles and impromptu games?
their jokes and their riddles and shouting of names?

did you enjoy school today?
their parents ask so hopeful

but with no double dutch
no hopscotch   jacks   or jump rope

where is the laughter
the magic
the reason for hope?

what becomes of a school house
where soul does not dwell?

when does the wind blow that lifts morose spell
and gives learning a chance to be loved?

we build more schools and more prisons too
in both places we sanitize away all truth

truth is not tidy or easy to predict
it smudges and grudges and speaks out of line
it stumbles and fumbles and throws quite the fit

truth is a young life allowed to encounter
its cry   dance   and holler

growing stalks need to touch one another
so as to confirm their growth

dubious shepherds with wicked sticks seek to tame
this growth by cutting down novice candlewick

earth has always born those who teach by
incarcerating
forcing children to learn by peaking through bars

we seek new script
pedagogy through humility
learning through boldness and lucidity

we ask once again
what becomes of a school yard with no living things?

we have made a decision
we will no longer participate in any demolition
of our young

from this day forward we demand that children
be allowed to leave their human fingerprints

everywhere.

8.22.08

Hardly anyone is in the courtroom this day
as she stands up to advocate for a life whose fate
depends on whose voice will be strongest

the willful judge is about to decree
when she   the advocate
says:

Your Honor
this child . . .

your . . .
honor this child

what did you say?

I said honor this child

with all due respect judge
you will not place him in a home
where prejudice toward his very being
gnaws at his self-love like rats
hidden in the walls
that visit him at night

you will not banish him to a program
that conceives of him as inherently flawed

as an ill-mixed clay fit only for pounding
on the table by angry hands

I will not go home tonight having stood here
and allowed this child to be dispersed
according to the law's discretion

when no one has previously shown
any just discretion in his unattended life

I will not go home and eat my dinner
and tuck in my children
and sleep sweet dreams

I will not return to the office tomorrow
and be greeted kindly by colleagues
as we collaborate with a system
on mediocre intervention
in frightfully troubled lives

or fail to intervene at all

I will not keep closed my mouth
as you render your judgment
as though finality has been passed

no child's life should ever be cast
in such abbreviated possibility

every single such life deserves and demands
the fullest amendments to its story
until we have arrived at a suitable plot
not concluding with a graveyard of desolation

hammer your gavel with all your might
find me in contempt because I am

I have contempt for this parade
of excuse and rationale

I have contempt for our blaring trumpets
of self-congratulation

I have utter contempt for our acceptance
of less than our best for *other people's children*

if not me
then who will stand up against hurtful laws?
who will risk losing his job
so a child won't lose her life?

I will
I will lose my job and take my scolding
but I will walk out of this courtroom
a human being who bent not before might

this child will see wrong turned to right
before you or I greet our goodnight

so your honor

honor this child.

10.5.07

Standing before congress the worker testifies:

ladies and gentlemen   as you appropriate
please remember

this child is not a grant   a request for proposal
a 10-year-study   a strategic plan
a child-centered community-based
culturally-competent rhetoric

this child is now   immediate   true
touched by plague of our own hollowness

we must serve this child now

this child is not a category   diagnosis
prediction   predicament   case
acronym for sin or surrender

is not a test score   performance   grade
pie chart   bar graph   point on the bell curve
outlier   mean   median or mode

is not cattle for prodding into a life track
and fattened with self-doubt for slaughter

is not a quota of outcomes
a trigger for funding renewal

this child is a banged up knee
a story still being written much less told

a footprint on Earth
a song in the wind
a blessing in the world
an anger at the mouth of our failure's cave

sorrow of a slave
revolt of servitude
uprising of dignity

a bloodied lip
a sassy input
a reminder   a warning
a beacon   a borrowed thing

a litmus   an escapee from our promises
a signpost   indication   night light
goose talk   North Star

reason   season   hope
checkmate on our spiritual board

this child is our absolute
and final frontier

we had better earmark
this young life as though it were
pumping oil out of its little heart
enough to satisfy our greed

forever.

4.17.08

At the staff meeting
the workers discuss their various
roles and responsibilities

midway through one worker interrupts
with a pensive voice:

we have neglected a priority item
failed to even include it on our agenda
the subject we must address
is that of our collective responsibility

I need no planner   scheduler   pen or pad
to write this down amongst my many tasks

I need a heart   a mind   a reason   the truth
I require faith and determination

our responsibility is the child
our role is to serve the child

we have one responsibility
one role

our job descriptions   titles   positions
are secondary

in many ways they are illusion
in this great and singular task

we are all vulnerable   needful
dependent souls tethered to each other

we are wet and soaking
in the same stream

the side stream of devalued
human beings

I would like to share a story

I left this little boy
a quick note on blue paper

it said:

before you were ever judged
by a person on this planet
you were judged to be
beautiful and worthy of life

the breath of life itself
was your entrance ticket
your stamp into the club

you were born worthy
you already passed your greatest test

something Great thought you priceless
enough to be created

the rest of your life is not an audition
it is a grand performance

you have already been chosen
to grace the stage

now dance sing
make your point to the world

we are not your director
we are your audience

Greatness Itself directs you
we can only witness and learn

I saw him tuck the note
in his pants pocket

I prayed it would not get
washed in the laundry

slowly
his demeanor changed over
the remainder of the school year

on the last day of class
he tugged at my arm
said he needed to talk to me

outside on the main entrance steps
he shared his secret with me   saying:

it has not been easy for me being in this place
all of you adults have different titles
which seems to make you pull on us
students in competing ways

you each take a chunk out of me daily
to feed your sense of control

I feel like a minnow pulled to pieces
by frogs who will not leave their lily pads
to join me in the water

I keep thinking that if they did join me
they could feel what it is like
for a minnow like me

when you gave me that note
I did nothing with it at first

I thought you were just another frog
preying on me with a note for a tongue

eventually I opened up the note
I read it and instantly I felt safer here
in this place where you are

not a predatory thing
but a big minnow
who actually wants to swim with me

I wish all the adults here would forget
their roles and titles
and remember me.

4.17.08

At the podium
on the stage
in the late evening of her retirement party

she graciously receives the applause
of family   friends   colleagues   and
students   present and past

her eyes still twinkle
after all the years

she speaks into the microphone:

tonight I wish to tell the truth

so much of this work we do
in caring for our children
becomes tainted with the lies we tell ourselves
so that we may retain a measure of dignity

tonight as you honor me
I feel it is only right that I honor
the truth of what I have been

so that who comes after me
might dare to attain a higher service

about midway through my career
a boy showed up in my class
about a week after fall term began

he wore blue shoes

his clothes smelled of urine each day
his hair was a matted mess

his breath stank   his skin was ashy
he was shy   quiet   withdrawn

each class subject I taught
he spent with his head down
drawing in his notebook

he ate his lunch alone in the cafeteria
the other children were not so much
mean to him as thoroughly uninterested

his build was lithe   emaciated
he ate little   always mumbling to himself
as he finished his food

I was concerned about this boy
my calls to his mother went unreturned

he walked to and from school
so I never saw her pick him up

I did not have to
but the truth is
I chose to conclude many things about this boy

finally I decided to visit his home
his mother invited me in

I sat on a sunken tattered couch
and drank the sun tea she offered

she said
I am so sorry I have not called you back
I have been afraid of what you might
have to tell me about my son

I know he is struggling at school
he comes home crying

our family has been through so much
these last few years

my son has had to bury his grief
so he can take care of his brothers and sisters

I work too much and my heart is frail
since I lost a child and my husband
in the same cruel moment

I have seen my depression become my son's
I am so scared and so lost
and feel I have let us all down

last week he came to me in my bedroom
I knew he heard me sobbing
the lights were low

he said
mom don't cry we're going to make it through

I'm sorry I have disappointed you at school
it's just so hard right now

none of the students like me
I don't like myself

the worst part is I can feel every single one
of my teachers not liking me too

if just one of them looked at me differently
I believe I would have air to breathe
when I go there

If I could breathe there
I believe I could grieve there
and let all my pain go

instead I hold it all day long
it is hard to learn like that

in that moment on that couch
I realized that I could have been
that one teacher to pierce his obstruction
and let in his breath

I could have stopped his suffocation
if only I had not concluded him
in such horrible ways

from then on I would choose to see him
more beautifully

that was the day I learned
a lesson I've carried all the way
up to this night:

our conclusions touch lives
and our touch is permanent.

4.22.08

I switched from morning coffee
to jasmine tea

my students
lives enflamed
needed a calmer me

on the patio at morning
I listed in my mind
all the reasons I do this thing

in moments of classroom entropy
I would need to retrieve that list mentally
staple my heart to it emotionally
recite it as prayer spiritually

at each day's end I would have found
at least one more thing to add to the list

it would serve as my evening meditation
my nighttime dream

in the morning of next school day
I would write it across
the tablet of my identity all over again

a walking   breathing list
of reasons why I do this thing:

because you don't
I do this thing

because you won't
I will this thing

I choose to sing
I serve to bring
their better nature into being . . . .

the list went on in endless verses
the greatest change occurred in me

my persona took on the soothing
calm of jasmine tea

now I was the soft soaked leaves
while before I was self-defeating rigidity

I had tried to get them to build model houses
with construction paper and markers
because it was *my idea*

they wanted to build their world
with paper clips   rubber bands
staples   popsicle sticks   and glue

now I was able to let them

they built something that grasped
stretched   bonded   bent   gripped
clamped   shone   leaned   folded   stood

they built a shrine to possibility

and I
I kept sipping my jasmine tea.

4.24.08

They emerge onto the track for gym class
traveling in tight groupings
like buffalo

even as they giggle   tease   taunt
scream   flirt   fight

I know they are unsure   uncertain
yearning   searching

each clumsy dare of selfhood
is followed by shy subtle glance
around parading herd for approval

daily without exception
they gain their measure of self and others

my own unsure glances
daring expression of being
can crush their tenuous hold
on this idea of who they are

some days even ants are larger
than how these calves see themselves

then day turns over to the next
they become inflated mountain
unpassable forest

their thoughts so lost
deep in the stand of their complexity
I can only guess what gathers by the fire
at the center of their woods

as they become us
trust is too much to bear
they need convince themselves
they are any thing but us
how else their dignity?

the games they play with each other
those between boys and girls
are not only games they practice
this is how they will treat each
other as men and women

for now though they play games
I stand in the middle
blow the whistle
announce the rules

when I dare to pass on to them
what I have learned about how
games turn into habit seeds
for joy and pain

when I dare to go there
even I have no idea how
I might have just changed
the games we play

for now
they scream at me demanding
that I call them beautiful

that I bow down and polish their brilliance
this the proof to them that I can see it

their defiance protests to me:
I am the one and only
I am something not seen before
and I will not be grouped

yet they are younger than the young trees
tender as april's leaves

they move down the halls
out onto the yard
joined at the elbow
in sheer trepidation

they are loud   mute   strong   vulnerable
powerful just enough to scare me
yet their heads hang down timidly

they are early expressions
on face of Earth so much older

this world is their prairie
they move as buffalo

we their bur or haven
terminal blaze across the grass
or watering hole of their dreams.

4.24.08

She is a farmer's daughter
and cannot help but relate her work to the land

at the town hall meeting she takes a stand:

This garden is not so easy
the carrots resist my pull

I tear my palms and fingers
yanking on green that shows
above dilapidated crust of soil

I am hoping root has gone to orange

I hope that when the thing I seek
gives up being buried
explodes from ground
the force will not send me tumbling

though it would be a blessed falling

this garden is not so easy
how hard are we willing to work to pull
certain children from ungiving ground?

is it true that every child is worth the same?

not in this world
but a place exists that counts worth differently

that place is where I pitch my tent
drive my stakes with a sturdy foot

place me in the schoolhouse
in the courtyard
on the dust named road

let my vessel there surrender
that which I cannot suppose

that sweeping arc of miracle
the long douse souls require

call my message what you will
place my lamp where you wish

the hungry will find their crumbs
the thirsty will have their drink

need will meet its truest love
in the fountain of my audacity

in the end I die of worldly values
find my blessings in shy and tepid creek

some go looking for bright coins
and stones in the water

I troll for camouflaged things
unseen against a dirty bottom

poured over and unmoving beneath
the dominant flow

I pull these things
out into evaporating air
where

striations and character in my palms
there begin to show

I blow
to further dry them off
my heart then a sufficient buffer cloth

I set them down on the old oak table

stand back a step or two

what once was blended into dirty bottom
now reveals its mystery true

these things are sedimentary stories
accumulated places of finest
silt and shredded fabric

these things are the cracked marble ball
a child treasures

these things a board with splinters
a leaky hull
moldy corner
moss at the foot of tree

these things the rain before we wake
leaving a wet grass
whose watering we did not see

these things the fruit within
the blossom within the bud
within the branch within the tree
within the sprout within the seed
within the soil within the earth
within the world within Creation

this is how we see

all that is great is born of small
all that is modest is the consequence
of what stands tall

this garden is not so easy
knees burn and stain of rocks and dirt
as we kneel shift lean
plant turn toil

this child began as a dream
in the girl who became a woman
then a mother   to this child

that child started as a song
in the boy who became a man
then a father   to that child

brittleness of spirit comes after
what comes before

first is the encounter with
what should not be

the child who encounters
is the tool for change

we have inserted her into
what should not be

now we must turn her
use her as a key

her wound   suffering   learning   healing   becoming
opens the door
onto the patio of what should be

we through a child's encounter
step out into sunlight

brown at the skin beneath
the radiance of
our human possibility.

4.15.08

Truth is
my mind is lashed to the idea that he
simply will not become something beautiful

at night I gnaw at the hefty rope
binding me to these disbeliefs

I pray that by morning
I will have chewed my way through

morning comes too soon
too many fibers remain intact

when I put on my clothes
for work I keep trying
to strip off the pessimistic cloak
that makes me a ghoul before him

he who is so young and not completed
he who washes his hair
in the dirty water
my mind's basin provides him

that water stains his scalp
penetrates his pores
becomes him

no wonder he only smiles
when he is being trashed by peers
their scathing confirms his impotence
strangely   we sometimes prefer
to be proven right about
painful self ideas

than to be proven wrong by artists
who paint our light

no wonder he cannot stand
to be in front of mirrors

he is looking to be not seen

as long as he believes he is monstrous
he will either seek to kill the monster
or he will do what monsters do

truth is I failed him
before I ever met him
when I let acrid wishes
from jilted grown folks
join my bones

now I stand in the rain
hoping something born of sky
will wash me out
and leech my bones
of their sour saturation

now I open my briefcase
search for a tonic I can drink
to give me drunken goggles

the kind that make what is unattractive
appear to be worth taking home

now I fumble in my purse
for a magic lipstick that will
force my mouth to smile at him

my purse is fat and overburdened
such lipstick is surely
at the bottom of my mess

truth is I used to be able
to love him

before I came to this
place that mocks my elders
who needed no such goggles
to fall in love

this place where flowers
go unfertilized
their tender waiting places
long unvisited by the
buzzing swarm of us who sentiment:

where are the better flowers?
the ones worth touching
with my belief?

truth is I am sick of my many
mental lashings

they actually make me sick

to spend my life in a valley
where my own thoughts fill
the skies with falling things

this is not the place
I wish to be

I want to lead the rebellion
drink from the courage cup
Mary McLeod Bethune
pressed to her lips

I have the power to resurrect
my affection

to let my enchantments
burrow deep

today I will chew through
the final fibers
let what sleeps come through

perhaps in dormancy
it will have dreamt a reason
for me to tilt my cup
into this child's heart

and pour.

5.28.08

Some people like to pet him
as though he is a subservient beast on four legs

others keep their distance
they are the eager scavengers swiping every
artifact from the ground of his world
as though each broken shard
is evidence of his inferiority

they take their trinkets
to the lab of their presumption
where they run lazy tests
on faulty machines spitting flawed algorithms

ultimately pronouncing this child's
being as carrier of a bubonic plague
or some such reason to quarantine
him behind plexiglass walls
of indifference or scorn or both

others eschew this dark archaeology
reasoning that if only the dust were
rinsed off the pieces
their idea of the artist would grow in esteem

these traitors to the caste system
sit close to the child
run their fingers through
his smooth ambrosia

this stroke releases his long encumbered
amber incense

precious collections left behind
by his hopeful ancestors
inside the far corners of his
fundamental chambers
commence to remember
they still have use

especially in this young and dying culture
these fine endowments shift and hum

once ruptured child becomes a chalice
his mind once barren shack
is now a palace
its walls ornate with masterpieces

child ablaze now surrenders his outer walls
moats and guards

lowers his ladders
extends his bridges

forest of the world around him
incinerates before his purpose born

what grows up after
through ash and haze
is a stand of believing trees

all because adults like you and these
sat close to him and ran your fingers
through his smooth ambrosia.

5.29.08

His inspiration comes from something
his great uncle said to him from a bowlegged
rocking chair on a weathered porch in august:

we have too many dams
not nearly enough rivers

it takes a broken heart
to unleash compassion's holy flow

we have too many dams and walls
too much hardness   toughness
callousness   smugness   arrogance

these separation walls keep us from love
our own love
the love of others

our world dies for lack of irrigation

a mighty generational river surges
bangs against our tall barricades
trying to break through

we have spliced it in contradiction
made it to snake down crazy canyons
narrow and shallow in the flats

no vital flow can follow our ill laid maze

we sit heavy and unyielding
on what we believe to be thrones of knowing

instead we are stuffing brilliance back down
into its disbelieving burrows

we reign over hollow kingdoms
nobody lives in the chateaus we pillory
with fantasies of domination and control

a small thing takes its drink
from the well in the courtyard
nervous and skittish that we will lance it from
the blind side for violating our code of ethics

a law that speaks of prohibition against
creative displays and the exercising of quirks
and talents not writ in the
Great Black Book of Normalcy

a small thing takes its drink
waits for the shadows to descend

who will be its protector?
whose heart will break enough
to be flooded with love?

1.20.08

How much breaking should
I allow my heart today?

which stories should I hold onto in a way
that leaves them bleeding all over me?

which ones should I wash away?

how human should I be
in the midst of this inhumanness?

they want me to make progress
in this teeming mine field

even as they harness my mine detector
with dictates of polluted politics

this child is given one oar
and expected to steer straight
on the boundless river

that one never sleeps
this one cannot stop sleeping

both are on the run from monsters
we have made

this one mourns her drinking father
as he plods on toward his grave

this one thinks she has to be
a woman for her siblings
peddles her body as we have taught

it occurs to me that I need to learn
something more about love
and how to deliver affection

for teaching rests on the ability to transmit
to a child that you care

I endeavor to become the village healer
who with mortar and pestle
grinds grandmother's herbs
into a potent salve to cure

this one's running nose
this one's busted upper lip
this one's stinking clothes
this one's front tooth chip

and to treat the blindness of the royal court
who fail to recognize

this one's regal posture
this one's royal ways

this one's dimpled smile
this one's downcast glance

and in each a shy romance

yes I take on the cloak of the sturdy ancestors
who simply chose as a matter of fact
to let their hearts break

all the way.

4.17.08

The new worker is charged by her supervisor
with creating her own professional pledge

she sits by a river and meditates
society leaves her thoughts
insight takes its place

she writes

My mantras:

smile at him for he may
receive none at home

respect him because I may be
his solitary oasis of esteem

forgive him because his landscape
is littered with bear traps
ready to punish him to the bone
for every slight misstep

expect of him   for his days
are a dark eclipse of non-expectation
let my faith in him be his light

let my persistent effort
be a tourniquet for his hemorrhaging
temptation to give up

teach him
in too many moments he is not being taught

translate his tongue
he speaks in low avoidant code
to conceal that he is afraid and unknowing

see beyond his mask
his hard outer shell protects
a tender flesh of heart

his apparent disinterest is his response
to a world that has been disinterested
in him

learn his story
it is my path to understanding his way
of existence

withhold judgment
he is the manifestation of every
judgment passed against him

share my story
it may be his first glimpse
of my humanness

provide him a room for laughter
in the home of our relationship

counteract every assault
on his dignity by taking a stand
that risks social disapproval
be his amazing grace

thank him silently for giving me
the opportunity to practice patience

do not ever stop excavating
until I reach the layer of his beauty

his sediment can wash me clean
if I learn how to sift it through my own

remember he is a social myth

daily build for him in my mind
a truth encrusted throne.

5.29.08

A cold wind blows
through the heart of those
who believe themselves free
in such a way they need not participate
in humanity

the cold therein steels the heart to harden
weeds grow where should be a garden

pardon never may come to those who run
from this final intimacy
this dissolving in the human sea

greedy be we who clutch ourselves closed
on crutch of homogeneity and similarity
based on fear and insecurity

the hurt we do is to ourselves and our kin
more so than to the quilt human and free

for who but Madness believes it may
separate its grain of dust from desert wide
its slice of water from ocean's bath

what soul shouts "I am"
but is not truly being
human
which is to say

we on this earth breathe not air
but one another
in isolation souls do smother

would we but dare to open up
joy's breath would fill our spirit cup

this social world is our drinking water
what fool pollutes her drink with prejudice
when she can purify it with tonic of her heart

relationship is our holy vessel
binding fast our vines to trestle

those vines be our generations
seeking bloom
our compassion heeds them room

our own children feel the stroke
of tender human spoke
on Creation's turning wheel

and bear us gifts by their becoming
not fractured souls but music humming

one day the song full and flush
but first compassion its seeds in us
to lay in music's underbrush.

8.03.06

Written and recited as part of a keynote for Children's Home
Society & Family Services All-Staff Day, Minneapolis, MN.

I have been taught an idea of him
that is a sin

it starts in his skin
snakes through his tongue
tinges the air with the song he has sung

and yet I was born with a heart
better than this
so I resist

I resist the talcum blanching of prejudice
my own people have taught this
idea of him

and though I love them   my own people
I will not betray his youthful right
to wear his skin and be treated

to the absence of my prejudice

so I resist

my colleagues clown his manner
of speech even as their whispered
viper hiss is an awful lisp

and though I would bypass social
friction if I were to join them in this

I will not let beat a single sounding
of my heart's malice
at his speaking of his native tongue

though generations spread
the weary myth of his subhumanness
I will not do this

I am pressed to judge him
in the context of his otherness

I will not
his beauty springs from the source
of providence

and though most are blind to the
genius of his expression

I will not hang his good works
in the closet of my shamefulness

his will go on my central walls of gallery
his notions will join my jubilee

and if a monarch butterfly should slide
down breeze to rest on me
I shall see him in that precious monarchy

as others sweep him into their noxious
mental cyst
I will lean him into a gentler mist

oh we callous calcified heart stained masses
we know not what we do

he is a notion brighter than all of this
his dying is our own in time
his glory slakes the world of thirst

I have pitched my splintered stake
in his unsung ground

and come the noise of lies to break him down
come this unspeakable mourning sound

I will resist.

6.1.08

He shares his dream with the group
near the conclusion of the retreat:

In my dream a child spoke:

"When you beheld me as a baby, as a newborn soul, my skin did not frighten you, nor did my voice, though as yet unskilled. Now as I stand before you, a child still, though larger, with voice more pronounced—now I am to you not something to be cradled and sung to, but a deviation from your comfort zone, to be controlled and scorned. I am only a child, and even though I may act out, I do so only as you do so, because I am uncertain of my role. Who am I—my teacher—that your adoration for me has grown so cold?"

the man continues:

These words captured me in a dream last night, and I was ransomed by the fright. For my freedom I surrendered blindness, and now I must ask myself this: What wicked wind has, as the child said, blown me so cold? Are not these children here, the ones I now fear, the same children whose infant preciousness gave me desire to swoop them up, diapers and all, and cuddle and cradle and kiss them without end?

This is what I believe:

I am a teacher, potent and proud. I am a teacher, a preacher, a listening ear. I'll not forget who I am, regardless the weather, regardless the tempest that churns in this dizzying world.

I am a teacher, potent and proud. And I must know that mine is not the task of imparting knowledge, but that of letting it bloom. Nor should I tarry too long on bending the young to kneel at my power. My true power, my given gift, is that of lifting up, not forcing a kneeling rift.

The daily frustrations at the hands of these young, I can recount easily in my sleep—the fighting, the disrespect, the absence, and lack of effort; the enduring sway of their emotional pain. But if I look closely I can see that their frustrations are truly mine, for their behaviors are only the outpouring of genuinely human needs. In their search for identity I see my own striving for a role amongst an increasingly unfamiliar student crowd. In their search for belonging, I too am reflected, for if I feel so at home, then why do I fight so hard to claim my turf? They are disillusioned, disheartened, and of low self-esteem. Their emotions are bottled up; they have no place to scream. But if these aren't also forces welled up in my own chest, then all my life has been but a dream.

Feeling inadequate to the task of rightly handling these Every Persons, and their cultural needs, my security is not adult-like; it is juvenile, it bleeds. How am I to be the gender, ethnic, linguistic, religious, and individual caretaker? These issues I have not even fully satisfied within myself, and so I seek shelter in what I teach. But what DO I teach?

We are teachers, potent and proud, but we must know our place, we must not crowd. We are the *fertilizer*, but not the *fertility*. The fertility is theirs because they are the Young. It is now their turn and this is their stage.

This too I believe:

I am the Black child's brother and sister. The Latino are mi raza, my race. I AM of the Asian persuasion. I am Russian, and an American Indian, and I . . . am all over the place.

The wheelchair-bound student over there near the stage, I must push, not against her chair, but against her spirit, to climb, to leap, to dare.

The young boy who speaks a language I cannot make out, I must understand that, far from being a threat, he is a whole new world to explore; here before me, without travel, a brand new shore.

I am all people at once, for to be culturally any of these, one need only be human first. The second need is simply to spend some time in a culture's midst. In this I am well qualified, because each culture that walks through my classroom doors, I breathe in as if it were air. Therefore, in essence, my hair is both straight and kinky, my skin both dark and fair.

To encounter such varied and wondrous new life, courageous curiosity has often in the history of our world had to sail and traverse, and climb, and battle, and freeze and starve. But here sit I, at the head of a frenzied court, while an endless stream of discovery places itself in my rooms, in my halls, in my hands. This unsettling time, burgeoning with unforeseen possibilities and visions, is not the time to wither away in fear. Nor is it the time to bellow an intimidating stand of power to allay the insecurities we find so hard to accept. We are teachers—sunshine sent to glare upon a vastly flowing garden. How dare we burn too brightly and make limp our tender youth? How dare we shroud them in the cold of our frightened stooping behind clouds of habit? We are the Sun, how could we so coldly dare?

As a teacher I also know this:

I am a teacher, and whether I ply my craft in the classroom or the lunchroom; whether with a globe or a lathe; with a beaker or a conductor's wand; whether I drive the bus, or counsel the troubled, or maintain the buildings, or monitor the halls, I am an adult in a land of children, and their eyes are upon me. I am teaching even when I know not that I am.

I must be thoughtful, quick-minded, curious, and pensive, as they are. I must be responsive, flexible, and ever-surprising, as they too are. I must learn, as they do. I must absorb and grow; and give some to get some, as I expect of them. To the extent that I demand their ear, I must also lend mine, for a child's worst fear is of the self's voice gone unheard. So I must gather their every word, and treat it as gold. I must make harvest of their words, in bushels of opportunity for growth. In doing so, I must show them how to make harvest of their own words, so they may become producers of the products we all consume in this world: creativity, skills, talents, insight, and achievements out of sight.

I must treat them each as dignitaries from their own unique foreign lands. The red carpet I roll out should be strewn with confirmation, expectation, and appreciation. My dignitary gifts should be wrapped in the provision that I will do all that I can to bring the world I know to them in a way that allows them to bring their world to me, and to their child peers. I will serve as a scaffold, a bridge, between what has been, for better or for worse, and what they will bring into being, also for better or for worse. They have as much right as all others who have trounced and tripped on this Earth to make their own footprints. If they be footprints of gold, or footprints unworthy, they will be THEIR footprints, for I will not have held them hostage in the sky, bound by my arms, left with feet dangling in despair. I will make them care.

I also know that if I do not give shelter with equal kindness to all of the children in these halls, I will have endangered myself; for when a child is harmed, with no remedy on hand, only negativity will sprout from the wound. So I must give voice to the voiceless, and I must have the security not to shrink from the unfamiliar languages, customs, and attitudes in my presence. I am a teacher, potent and proud, and I will have the strength to recognize that the very forces I fear, these children fear too. Their troubles and struggles are born of that brew. If I expect that they come correct to my table, then I must ask: How have I cleansed my own hands? I am bound to shed hypocrisy by scrubbing more heartedly at the dirt I carry—my harmful views, which were fostered by my own unheard, unexplored childhood truths.

If not for the world that my children, and their children will occupy, then FOR myself I must no longer TO myself lie. I am a teacher, and so I must teach, I must reach . . . the hearts of these students here. Soon they will either ascend to positive adulthood, pulling me up alongside, or they will descend into adulthood's dungeon of despair, and pull me down too, for they will have no care.

I must cleanse from my heart the negative pulses. I know they can sense my true pulse like a strong scent on my skin. So I will do this thing—I will teach, I will preach, I will reach their hearts and make them stand tall in their childhood land. I will face honestly my faults, and not beat myself down. Like them, I am a child in the sense of my tenure in this new world of theirs; and I will misstep, but at least I will have stepped at all.

I will do this because I am a teacher, potent and proud, and mine is the doorway through which I must let *all* children pass. My potency will uplift them, and as they triumph, so shall I. As they find their place in the world, so shall I know mine. I will teach because I am a teacher, and I must.

I *must* teach.

4.18.95

At the head of the path that leads through the woods
slender boy runs up to the playground monitor
his voice too worn for his age:

will you walk me home?

sure son
so did you have fun in school today?

my uncle beats me
my auntie plays with my no-no places

paralyzed for a moment by the sheer
overwhelming scope of this truth
the man stops   searches for words

not knowing what else to do
he places a gentle hand on the boy's shoulder
they walk to the ice cream parlor
and talk baseball and girls

it is all he can offer in that moment

it is more than has been offered
to a slender boy all day

hurt is paved over in a fine dusting of reprieve
the moment though fleeting is priceless
a reservoir of joy to be dearly recalled
in the long moments to follow.

4.17.08

It is a conference for adults
who advocate for disconnected youth

the opening speaker begins to recite a recipe
for what youth need
saying:

Our children need a place to call home

just then a youth in the audience
rises and says:

excuse me but I've been thinking

in the garden
by the brook
a thought came to me
and once settled took

you who work on my behalf
also need a place to call home

you need a running stream
in the form of lasting connections
to those with whom you toil

you need loving families
circles of associates
in the office and on the road

you need colleagues who care
for you and dare to lift your load

the price you pay for this mission
is steep indeed

you need supportive peers
to polish your tarnished shine
especially in the winter of a nation
whose warmth has withered on the vine

you too need a safe place to live
for while you work and give
your spirit is a tender thing
that needs and hurts and *is*

someone needs to help you learn
to take good care of yourself

we youth cannot afford
for your wellness to lose its light
we need your strongest flame on our behalf
your brightest glow for this precious fight

the way you do this work
should not leave your soul impoverished

your days should be built on bricks
of relationship that bring assets to your life

all the ideas you generate to usher us
toward our golden potential gate
should shine on us in such a way
that they reflect off us
and shine on you
deepening the cup of *your* dignity

where has frivolity fled?
I cannot find it in your eyes
you've lost the happiness
you meant to share with
the very youth that now
walk eclipsed in your shadowed song

you've not done wrong
you've just lost your way
your compass of identity
is rusted and nearly broke

remember you came into this
because you dared to dream
of a greater bliss for those like me

it is time to stop and drink
from a cleaner water
refresh your inner spring

there is such a thing
as suffering the cruel offspring
of a nation's negligence

and fighting with due diligence
for justice for our youth
while still managing to grasp and cling
to the very thing that lets you sing

the soul inside
the softer hide
the fertility for your merriment

never ask where happy went
it never goes away

it just grows discouraged
when our heart open
is pierced and then
our joy leaks out
hope loses hold
and fears of old
rise up to block the light

never ask where happy went
joy is a seed that grows in the soil sold
to a life devoted to humanity

joy once was a sunflower standing tall
watered faithfully joy can live again

a child is not the only one
who needs the caress
of a loving summer sun
you who toil need this too
a social family of caring folks
where celebrated spirits roam

in the garden
by the brook
a thought came to me
and once settled took

adults too need a place to call home.

1.27.08

Written for a keynote presentation for the National Network for
Youth Annual Symposium.

An elder woman sat me down to talk
she noticed the fatigue pulling at my face

she said no no
don't you give up on me now
don't you go to sleep on me
on them
you're almost there
you've come too far

her skin was beautifully wrinkled
portraying the terrain of her life

her hair wonderfully grayed
so it could reflect the sunlight
and share that illumination with others

her eyes magnificently clouded with cataract
so she could see with a higher vision

she said
youngblood
I have seen a better day on down this dust caked road
I might not get there with you but I know a way

she said
when the children are scattered
gather them up

when families are in jeopardy
lift them up

when communities are in disarray
find the courage
take matters into your own hands
mend the fabric

when the sky grows dark
seek not shelter from beyond yourself
but seek it from within yourself

I asked her
dear ma'am
how do we accomplish this?

she said
very simply
you all got to accumulate your wisdom

wisdom
that sweet nectar of life
that drips down the vines of generation
and percolates through the pores
of mothers and fathers
and comes to rest upon our lips
where if only we open ourselves
we may taste of it

and become whole again.

4.13.00

I

being a teacher
forewent the temptation to judge
instead huddled myself behind the visage
of spirits dancing

caught the brilliance of their surges and rhythms
and like a visitor from a distant place
beheld this obvious expression of a Great artist

then breathing more deeply
eyes blinking to confirm my sight
form began to coalesce around these spirits

I beheld them as children
early-life beings I knew well from my days

but these
I saw in new light
with Creation Itself emanating from the very
breast of them

I realized their dance was rightful to them
as were their smiles

so too the wisps of translucent color drifting
tendrils from their bodies

I knew these silken wanderings as dream states
for they carried concentrations of a most
intensified light:

ebbing balls of imagery and affection
they found their way to the ceiling
there clouding over us as confection

In this moment I was thankful
of my initial hesitation to judge
to judge the frantic darting about
the chattering buzz   piercing screams
belly laughter   pushing   pulling

tugging   leap-frogging
piggy-backing   karate-chopping

crying pouting   name-calling
hand-holding   why-the-sky-is-blue?
we missed you

for here were bulbs of midday brightness
cloaked in gangliness
costumed in cloth of hope-to-be
scattering in their movement toward sky

never again would I witness this dance
and see not first
their spirit core fluttering about

fireflies dominating their outer forms
weaving wisps of imagery in dream above
to sweetly dust the day.

7·7·97

On twin swings
they breeze back and forth side by side
woman and girl

the younger says in a canary's voice
close your eyes . . . okay . . . now . . .

do you see me?
If so you seed me   I take root in you

do you feel me?
if so you feed me
I fill my well with water clean

do you hear me?
if so you heal me

understanding is the medicine I need

will you be my student?
if so I will teach
and in teaching I will learn from you

in marriage two make a sacred pledge as one

in this relationship we cannot be one
without a pledge from two
that you will seek my magnificence
and I will seek yours too.

3.12.04

A version of this poem was published previously in Jaiya John's
book *Beautiful*.

She
skips rope to the beat
of chocolate milk surging
down a parched 12-year-old throat
in high July

her
bare feet bouncing for relief off the street
heart beat moving fleet
dreams dancing in her head
of when her family will be whole again
because she feels

if
we can just get it
together we'll be okay
cause we are family
can't nobody take that away from us
can they?

that night
in the glow of street light
hidden under the sheets
she takes pencil to paper
feeds her journal these words:

my greatest fears:

she writes
and as she writes the words
are also written on the blackboard inside her mind
etched on the inner walls of her heart

where they will stay
stubborn graffiti
hidden in the shadows
but persistent all the same

and she writes

my greatest fears:

Mommy dying
Daddy crying
bad things under the bed
somebody taking my family away
away

I know a way to keep bad things away
I'll pray
I'll do like Ms. Johnson at the library
when people come at her mean
I'll look at them scary
I'll build a wall around my heart
that way no fires can start inside my chest
that would escape from there
and burn the rest of me

I'm afraid cause people
don't seem to like my family
they don't say so with their mouths
they speak it with their looks
wish I had me some cookbooks
for all the crooks who come to steal our joy

I'd make me up a meal so hot and spicy
they would have to ask us for water
least for once they'd be asking *us* for something

seems like we're always asking
somebody else for something

then they always give us that look
like we are something less
and they are something more
but they don't know my godmother
she can sing like an angel
they don't know my
best friend Keisha
can't nobody add
numbers as fast as she can

they don't know my Uncle Roy
I've seen him make a gourmet meal
from nothin' but flour and water
seem like to me

my Daddy he may not be fancy
but he can dance with Mommy
real sweet and make her feel like
somethin' special when he dips her down

and Mommy she may not have
all the best dresses and shoes
she may not talk smart-like
but she knows more ways to
stretch a dollar than those folks
in suits and nice cars always
stressin' they budget and fussin'
'bout they stocks and *bombs*

and my family
we sure can tell some stories
keep you laughin' most the night

stories 'bout folk we know
and some we don't
don't wanta know either
and stories 'bout Moses
and Ms. Harriet Tubman
and Jesse Owens
stories that make you feel
good about yourself
yeah we can light a fire
with stories and keep the house warm
'til morning light

I just hope nobody ever takes me away
cause how would I ever find my way back
and why are people always talking
about sending me to a better life
folk seem awful comfortable
with the idea of me never seeing
my family again

I read my books
I remember they used to do that
to slave children
send them away to a better life
I bet in the Master's house
when trouble came
the children didn't get sent to a better life
seem like folk think children like me
weren't ever supposed to be with
their own families in the first place

yes'm
I read my books
they took certain other children away too
they called it making them civilized

they used to cut off all their hair
us   they take us and cut off our memories

but what if I don't want no better life?
what if I just want *my* Mommy
and to play with *my* brother
and keep going to *my* school
and never ever split up with *my* friends?

so what Mommy's not doing well
I'll go stay with Big Ma
she loves me too
and if not Big Ma
more than two people in my family love me
ain't that true?

I get so tired I just want to sleep
and wake up and us have everything we need
I don't need another family
I just want people to stop being so mean to us
it makes my Daddy cry

now that Ms. Tina
from the agency she for real
I'll tell you how I know
most folk don't look me in the eye
when they speak to me
I mean they do
but really they just lookin' right past me
like I'm a ghost or something
and they just talkin' to the wind

Ms. Tina she looks me in the eye
I can feel her gaze settle on my soul

and when I speak or even when I don't
I can *feel her* listening to me
now that's some real stuff

yeah Ms. Tina
she's not like some other folk
I've even seen her look at Mommy
like Mommy's a real person
Ms. Tina don't know
but after she leaves
Mommy floats around the house
like a queen or something
I like that cause I don't
think most people see Mommy's beauty
does being poor make your beauty
invisible?

Ms. Tina she talks to Daddy
like he's a full grown man
not a boy
seem like if you're a man like Daddy
in this world
if you stand up all the way they beat you down
and if you crouch down
they smile and pat your back
Daddy wasn't made for that I don't think
but after Ms. Tina leaves I notice Daddy
treats Mommy better
heck
he treats us all better

Ms. Tina she don't know that

it must be hard for Ms. Tina
working with all these families like ours

cause it seems she don't have much support
some days I see her dragging her spirit around
behind her like it's about to fall off
in the dirt and get lost

I wonder if a spirit is like an umbilical cord
wonder if you cut it loose
does it shrivel up and die
hope I never see that happen with Ms. Tina
cause then who would treat us right?

and who's gonna believe in us?
I think it hurts a soul a whole heap
to have the whole world not believe in 'em
except for one person

wonder if that's what Jesus felt like
when they strung him up on the cross
poor Jesus
he didn't have no Ms. Tina by his side

sometimes I feel like everybody wants to
crucify our family for being the way we are
like we did something wrong by not having
money and for making mistakes
don't the people who get to keep their children
make mistakes too?
who's there to scold them?

I remember the time Ms. Tina thought
Ricky and me might have to get put
with another family
or at least in another home
I remember how she sat with us
and made us call all the relatives together

to talk and figure out what to do
I remember how she kept asking
us about our strengths
I thought she meant who had the most muscles
later I realized she meant how did we
deal with our troubles

she kept pushin' at us and pushin' at us
trying to help us help ourselves
eventually we found a way
for Ricky and me to stay in the family
while Mommy got better
Auntie Ruth took us in for a while
but at least my nightmare never came true
they never took my family away

but you know what?
I do believe that if ever Ms. Tina
had to put Ricky and me in another family
I do believe she would pick a good one for us
not any ol' family
I trust Ms. Tina cause
I think we mean something to her
most people when they come in our house
they look around and start frownin'

Ms. Tina
she comes in and her eyes always light up
when she sees us
I don't know if she's just fakin'
far as not likin' what she sees around the house
cause our house   there's not much in it
but at least she cares enough about
our feelings to fake like she's happy to see us
at least she cares enough to act like

we mean something
that's more than we're used to

but Ms. Tina
I think she really does care
if I was the people running the agency
I'd pay her a million dollars
cause that's what she's worth

every time I sleep through the night
and wake up and my nightmare
hasn't come true
that's when I think Ms. Tina
is worth more than gold

when I grow up
I'm going to make something
with my life
just so I can turn around
and thank my Mommy and Daddy
and Ms. Tina
the three big people
who always made me feel like I
was the sunshine
even when the rain was making them wet

Ms. Tina
I know I don't appear to be friendly
on the surface
but that's just cause I'm scared
that if I smile
that's where the pain will sneak in
and come back to visit my heart

she turns the page in her journal
and writes these last words:

my greatest fears:

Mommy dying
Daddy crying
bad things under the bed
somebody taking my family away

p.s.
Ms. Tina:

someday I'm gonna help all the
children just like you do
you ain't just my hero
you're my angel too

you take good care of yourself
I need you to

12-year-old closes her book
emerges from under the sheets
drifts off to sleep
as fireflies mimic the stars

nightmare chased away for
yet another night.

6.12.01

Previously appeared in *Beautiful*.

Her supervisor hands her a card celebrating
her one-year anniversary on the job

initially the young lady had been unsettled
that her work with adjudicated youth
escaped the neatly outlined ideas of her
graduate school textbooks
and ran into the margins in bright red scrawl

with her supervisor's patient guidance
she had grown into the reality of textured lives

the anniversary card reads:
the soul of social work is compassion
not passion   knowledge   experience

but compassion
the capacity and habit of wishing for others
that they do not suffer
then acting on that wish

this habit takes work   thus the term social work
not social games   social exercise or social hobby
social work

casually interested folks need not apply

all praise to the *work* in *social*
and to the souls who do the work.

1.31.07
Inspired by the impassioned comments of a social worker friend.

At the parent-teacher conference
she makes a promise:

I will not train them to test
I will nurture them to grow
for life's true tests care nothing
for multiple choice questions
or fill in the blank supposition

if I do not teach them to learn
and to love learning

to imagine   believe   forgive
remember   receive   honor
respect   dare   delight
dance   sing   sorrow
surrender to silence

if I do not teach them *all* of this
I lead them only to slaughter
fattened on synthesized pastures
of standardized grain

life's challenges care nothing for standards
they come at us in waves that mock
the tests for which we prepare our children.

9.7.08

My heart speaks now to you
the one who would serve to toil
on my behalf

I am the child of your daily labor
of your nightly dreams
let me show you something

but wait   I must warn you
what is to be seen lies this way
far within my private garden
in the depths of my treasure chest

come unto me but come unto me true
to venture here you must walk naked
and crying for no cloth must mask your
own frailty
tears must cleanse you well
lest you infect my soul
the very thing you
dare invite yourself beside

I have stories for you
they begin like this:

you see me as small and weak
yet my spirit is the ocean
my tide has crept along your shore

I have witnessed your secrets
you bear them alone and shivering

your garden has gone cold
but now is the season in which
you will choose to die or to live

know that this choice is my fate too
as you die or live I die or live with you

our spirits are bound as such
at night you cry out to God
why have you done this to this poor child?

you do not hear God's response:
what I have done to this poor child I too
have done to you

my own cry is different in those same nights
I cry *God why have you done this*
to the grown ones who toil for me   the child
that they cannot see my Truth?

so you see   we are two souls
each crying for the other
forming rivers of tears that
go ungathered

your garden has gone cold
the chill wilts my youthful flower

you cry for me yet your own struggle
steals my sunlight

it is time for you to release your cherry
blossoms and cloud the sky

what then rains down will cleanse your
vision and you will see me true

you will see that as you question
why you do this work
my child heart questions
why you began this work

whose life you serve in bearing this work
when will you at last betray this work
and therefore betray me

you will see that though you have
seen me as poor and pitiable
I am rich and blessed

you see my family roots as rotten
but fail to see that we are a worthy
tree that feeds on rotten ground

your heart loves me but your mind
judges me

you see my chocolate skin as
evidence that I come from something
burnt and broken

so you dream for me of places
bright and distant

my roots are not burnt or barren
only brushed and blemished
yet firm and fertile
my family still has beauty left to forge

you despair about my well fare
I wonder when you will say fare well

stress is a storm sweeping
your valley into dusk
my future in your hands
is your own sunrise

what you touch in me in winter
becomes my gift to you in June

you fear you make no change in
my life
but you forget the darkness
you keep from my life

you suffer a starving pocket
paid light of coin for your work
yet are made rich every moment
of this mission
you look for your payment
in the wrong purse

you spin webs of gold on the fabric
of our childhood futures
but look for fool's gold in false streams

your heart desires approval for the
battles you fight
look to your own echo for that
we create the world in which we live

you wonder how much you can afford
to bleed for me but
your blood is your own salvation

we eat the fruit of seeds we sow
child welfare is a harvest of faith
its true rewards run latent   blossom later

as I grow into the adult who raises
a family like the ones you dream for me

so here we are together
you wish beauty upon me
you *are* the beauty upon me

you have not only come to me
I have come to you
your work is my ministry
your love is my bread
your endurance my breath
your desire my warmth

your pain my hope
your courage my strength
your tears my drink
your nightmares my audience
your faith my shelter

I am your child
but here in my garden you are *my* child
I give birth to your glory
every day that I live

now you see me   don't you?
good   because that is why you are here

this is why we bleed
so that we may send our cherry blossoms
to the sky.

3.12.04
Appeared previously in *Beautiful*.

You
are the ones asked to step into heartbreak
and break no hearts
especially not your own

you are expected to step into private lives
and gain the trust of people
for whom trust has long since departed

you're the ones who have to
find a way to bring parenting skills
to people who see you as a stranger
trying to teach them a class
they never signed up for
and what's more
feel they already have a degree in

you're the ones who have to
make decisions that bleed
and then defend them to
those who were never there
to see the truth of these families

you're the ones charged
with keeping a family together
when society screams out
take those children away from there

you're the ones responsible
for placing children out of home
when society screams
keep that family together

you're the ones expected
to keep everyone dry
regardless the weather

it's you who is told
to go make sandcastles
out of mud puddles
and don't drag any of
that dirt back to the office
much less home with you at night

it's you who has
this much time
this much energy
and this many resources
to take on this much pain
this much fear
this many families
this many dreams
and turn it all into a happy ending
before this much spirit dies and fades away

I know you

I saw you creeping down by the river
one night
leaving your footprints in the mire
as you screamed at the water
and waited for the waves
to grow angry and swallow you up

I saw the smile on your face
and the celebration in your heart
when the family you worked with

discovered that they were valid
valuable
and held Divine light
and the Divine right and responsibility
to come together around a child

I saw the tension leave your body
and the relief come calling
both in the same breath
when you saw that the child placement
you made had grown blossoms
and was reaching for the sky

I've seen you in your moments of doubt
why am I doing this
your moments of joy
that's why I'm doing this
you're moments of quiet pride
this child is our future

I know you

you give us hope
you give us life
for a child is life
and the path between chaos
and freedom
contains a point of birth

you are that daring midwife
that sweet vicious Harriet Tubman
that uppity Nat Turner
humble proud angry
loving enduring
never relenting

always repenting
emergency rescue unit
without the uniform
paycheck
status
flashing lights

all you do
is get up off the canvass
and win your fights

Glorious
Godly
Goodness
your name is Grace

I know you.

6.13.01

He wants to remind himself of the need
for humility when anger or expectation
would be the easier thing

so each morning he reads to himself
the note that he keeps on his mirror:

I am not here to change him
but to be changed by him

in allowing him to touch my soul
I will have evidence of my success
success in getting out of the way
of his Divine becoming

by standing in the middle of his stream
letting him witness how he touches me

I must let him be audience to his greatness
impacting me

he is a home-bound comet shower
pocking my surface with beauty marks

entering my atmosphere
he blazes   trailing sparks

and I open-mouthed
amazed as he showers the sky
with the brilliance he brings to me.

8.19.08
Inspired by a good man with a tender heart.

Though he has been the child's advocate
he is surprised when the boy asks him:

will you come to my game?

sure son but won't your father be there?

yes

and your brothers and sisters?

yes

your friends?

yes

so I am curious why you care so much
about me being at your game

because you always stand up for me
even when it means risking your job
not many people take a chance on me
I figured you must believe in me
to do something like that

and I thought
if you can take a chance on me
I can take a chance on life

I figured if you are at my game
I will remember your courage
and I won't be afraid to take the shot.

9.4.08

Dear Administration
with these words I pen
to you my retirement letter:

my tears tattoo the mountains
of my paperwork now abandoned
in your catacombs of files
never again to see the light
of consideration or review

entombed more finally than a
royal family inside audacious crypt

my tears tattoo my paperwork
their long trails announcing
like warrior paint across my cheekbones
my every good intent
to prevent tragedy to my village

to beat back what aggresses
against our children

and yet as I walk on hard earned
calluses into vague cloud of my
what comes next
I am deeply vexed
my years of service have brought me this:

what aggresses against our dearest young
is neither external nor unannounced

indeed it lives within

our laws are serpentine
their consequence snakes avoidant path
around our young

a drunken delta of tributaries
that deliver any good they hold
to the ocean of adult cares

they finger from lofty plateaus
of lobbyist lips down the slopes of policy

landsliding over saplings
with rippling brutal force
unbridled on their course
to making someone grown content

perhaps paying handsomely those
who see the angle

our young all around them seeking water
little of it reaching them at the root

too much deviation for law
to reach its good intent

too many pockets padded along the way
too many things we truly value
wars and sports and celebrity
diverting the course of funding

too much noise in the law's conceiving
too much agenda
a dearth of grieving

far too many *can'ts* when a worker
wants to say *I can*

too many rants when a worker
took off on conscience   dared and ran

too many scoldings when protocol
is duly breached

too many casualties of neglect
washed up on eclipse beach

time was when I believed change
could come in increments

it can though rarely in time
for the child who needs it

now I believe in revolution
the only force strong enough
to decimate foul tradition at its root

if what kills children
is only partially destroyed
it grows new strangling weeds

and so I leave my files to their dust
and fate

lubricate my rusted hinges
swing open this work cage gate

and march myself into retirement
which for me shall be
a meeting with my inner authority

I will take my assignment with newborn glee

and sniff the subtle wind of my community
for aroma I should follow
until I find a few simple souls with hearts of courage
to do the thing a child needs
in that very same moment the child bleeds
no excuses   no misdirection

we of meager means and salty predilection
will join hands

walk into the burning building
somehow find the child
bring her out

turning round to face the flames
we will die to put them out

our souls the seeping sieve
we will die before we let
this burning live.

6.1.08

On the first day she writes her name
in fine form in white chalk
on the licorice colored blackboard

good morning class she says
pointing to her name on the board
I am ms. taylor

she spends that first day telling stories
of her wonderfully imperfect childhood

her students respond with a hesitant
blend of wit and bashful silence

on the second day a small child
strides to the front
picks up some chalk and writes:

my name is acacia

on the third day a wispy one
comes to the board and writes:

my name is nathan

this continues by the day
seemingly without conversation
a new child stands and walks
and writes and declares a name

the walls grow lush with vines of testimony
written in washable script

that's not all that happens

as the names begin to fill the board
the children start to reach beyond
name and pronounce themselves
more completely:

I am the defender of my territory

my love maintains the peace

I will never betray my family

my heart's pool has no bottom

your stories are safe with me

my every step is toward a better world

the writing escapes the blackboard
takes over the walls in a thick ivy
of exclamation

all because she introduced herself.

6.1.08

La pregunta:
por que hacemos esta cosa
porque

por los que lloran en la noche
por los que sueñan por la mañana

por los corazones que transportan
fealdad y belleza

por el rio que corre entre cada niño
un rio con hambre por almas florescentes

y porque hoy se casa
con ayer y mañana

y porque el cielo
y la tierra estan mirando

y cuando el pajaro
canta de felicidad
los niños oyen

y cuando podemos ver
la sonrisa en el sol
al primer momento del dia
podremos creer que
todo es possible para ella quien
tiene Fe

y cuando la bella luna dice
mirame mirame
no tengan miedo

tengan paciencia como yo
los niños son arboles
un dia que viene altos
pero este dia pequeños y en sus manos

y cuando nos veamos en el futuro
podremos decir
en este dia yo di
todo lo que soy a este niño
ahora un hombre
un arbol alto
quien besa cielo.

6.7.08

This poem came to me in Spanish originally, as imperfect as is
my Spanish. I then shared with a close Spanish-speaking friend
and *legendary* educator the English words that I intended for the
Spanish version to accurately represent. He graciously corrected
the Spanish version for me. The English version follows.

The question:
why do we do this thing
why

for those who cry in the night
for those who dream in the morn

for the light inside the pain

for the hearts transporting
ugliness and beauty

for the river that runs between every child
a river hungry for flowering souls

and because today marries
yesterday and tomorrow

and because the sky
and the earth are watching

and when the bird
sings of happiness
the children are watching

and when we can see
the smile in the sun
at day's first moment
we can believe that
all is possible for she
who Believes

and when brilliant moon says
look at me   look at me
do not fear

have patience as I do
the children are trees
one day to come   towering
this day   small and in your hands

and when we see each other in the future
we can say
on that day I gave
all that I am to this child
now a man
a tall tree
who kisses sky.

6.7.08

This is the English version of the preceding Spanish poem.

He writes the words as a conclusion to his
self-evaluation report:

This is why I teach . . .

we believe criminals crawl out
of the woodworks

we say they are a separate breed

no
they crawl out of childhood
kin to the best of us

our young who we abandon
greet us later in wearier skin

their smirk is borrowed
from previous wearers of longer femur
thicker conclusions
bone plates through with transformation

their idea of limitation is drawn
from rancid well water of grown folk
minds gone stale and bordered

their self-regard drips of sour sludge
from stalactites seeping down
inside our cavernous pessimism

they suckle the teat of our gloom

those who hunt us do not materialize
like condensation on the drinking glass

they become   steadily
a disordered calligraphy
drawn in slurred lines
ushered by our nervous tremors

there comes a point when a frightened
soul must take a stand

and so before too many poisoned minds
lock up our young with cryptic ciphers
I will steal their alphabet
drown their social ideas
in the mangrove swamps
where they can become detritus
as is their only merit

a long sojourn along prayer flag roads
on blustery mountain sides
brings me to a cave of blackened roof
distal ashy fire illuminating
dancing figures on the walls

here is where I draw my conclusions
against this chalky rock I practice
my drawing strokes

I begin a novice
leave not yet a master

come down from the heights
to write a feel good story
into flesh and bone
of these early prophets each

I strip ancient sinker cypress
lifted from swamp and bog
now hard and heavy
perfect for a writing instrument
that will not break

I unroll sheets of bamboo paper
with fledglings by my side
we write together stride for stride

we become florid rhythm
our strokes take to the page
soak the fibers until
a rebellious vocabulary
spills out   a stunning mural in bright relief

because I have not let the false translators
dictate this long love letter to our young
these adolescent seekers leave behind
the contaminants that breed
in wet dank despair

now they have an entire manuscript
fit to publish to a world of readers
a market famished for their genius composition

stained bamboo lodges in their teeth
they grin goofy nonetheless

this is why I teach.

6.11.08

His conscience shows up in his dreams
as a drill sergeant berating him for this tendency
to see his students through stereotypes:

Is your corpus callosum finished
passing nonsense back and forth yet?

myths run through that curtain
mice scurrying nowhere
leading you everywhere but to understanding

choose a hemisphere
discover its full stash of notions
then select the other
become friends with what it whispers

once you have become acquainted with the
persona of shadows you can tease out the light

then the veil splitting your brain as a mischievous
membrane can be free to be a bridge

your epiphanies can cross back and forth
after partying on both sides

this is better than when your rascal misbeliefs
darted between rationale and passion
your fear patrolling the crossing place
a hairy rebellious troll

seeing a young life clearly requires
this kind of meditation.

6.18.08

Since she loves the ocean her sister suggests
a way for her to relate to the defiant youth:

Be water
seep into the creases of his stone resistance
expand into the crystalline
of your most beautiful nature

burst him open
let him weep into fragments and shards

that he may be made whole again

let his granite crumble
his agate ore be revealed

let him return to sand
and discover how it feels to be
finely crushed coral
lovingly bedded into silt
by boundless affections of the sea

be water to him
let him return to the sea.

6.19.08

She writes a poem in response to her sister's urging:

I wade uncertain into cold broad sea
at foot of naked dawn

this child's life rises around my ankles
clenches tighter with every timid
step I take

steadily sinking into sediment others
have laid down inside his heart

two realities exist in this water

the one above
the one beneath
where organic neglect steeps and grows

I leave his shoals
wade unknowing into his wide waters

shelves exist beneath his surface
at any step I might encounter one
plunge down into his deep

suddenly come face to face with
the shadows and strange creatures
who inhabit his dark
untouched by the light of love

surely they are there
those creatures

those misunderstood things
that we call monstrous
swimming in his abyss

I wade in his waters

I get wet
dampened at the hem of my own heart
when perhaps I would rather remain
dry and farther up on the shore

his life is most truly lived out there
in the deep where he treads water
with a rowdy school of peers

sometimes their bared teeth
I take as mockery

that is before I see the foreboding
fin sweeping swiftly toward them
in the waves

then I am reminded that their bared teeth
are the horrified grimace of lambs
at the mouth of the opened gate
we should have closed on our shift
that does not end

and now the wolves descend from the hills
all burl and brawn
salivating at the opportunity to snatch
such a trembling and vulnerable flock
while still young

and now the night owls cry an early alarm
for it is not near dusk but rather fat of day
yet so brazen are these predators

they close in on a prey whose shepherds
would rather not
wade in the water

and so I gather whatever kindling lies
scattered across the floor of my courage

I light a fire   a torch   a brave candle
of faith and fortitude
that cannot be doused by such a thing
as treachery in the water

I gather what I can
take a deep breath
submerge myself

into this child's deepness.

7.30.08

If I have a prayer to keep me earnest
in this work often done in corners and shadows
alongside cliff sides of fear and
steep slopes of shale loosening and lifting

if I have a prayer to keep me earnest
it is that I might find the will
to dissolve myself into this service of souls

become smoke from compassion's candle
achieve absolute annihilation of my ego
before this monumental task

I pray that I may find the rough rock of reason
against which to shed my skin of insecurity

that a hard and persistent rain will fall
to loosen the soil of my ideology

that new understanding will receive the chance
to penetrate the surface of my *expertise*

that a knowing light will infiltrate
the burrows where sleeps my soul

a light so undeniable and burning
that my mind will be bleached
of all I thought I knew
making way for a fresh tablet to be inscribed
one whose words never completely
settle in the stone

I pray for the vagrancy of my devotion
to find a lasting home
perhaps in the nest that is my purpose revisited
daily   hourly   by the moment

I pray to become a beacon atop a lighthouse
on the hill of humility

forever looking up in admiration at this
vast array of children strewn across the sky

that they might always locate North Star
shining through my nothingness

and remember their way onward
to a glory that they own

and when august days burn a hole in my unsure chest
leaving a geyser of ambivalence to come gushing out

and I doubt   pout   reconsider whether
I shall tread this road for another year

I pray for a tear
that would fall from the heavens
penetrate the abiding mist
splash over my aching
make all things clear
brush me with a whisper
to leave with a child:

be still my beloved
I am near.

7.30.08

I dreamt one night that I was a requisition form
for services one of my youth clients dearly needed

I was a floating waif
a wispy sheet of desires
tattooed in printed words describing
what one child's life required

I drifted down a dark hallway
staring up at blinking popping fluorescent lights

moving past co-workers in conversation
I caught a downdraft
landing on the first of a long series of desks
where I awaited a signature from each

after leaving my worker's hands
I landed in the supervisor's basket
she was on vacation so I remained
for seven and one half days

next the desk of the assistant program manager
she had issues with a certain omission
from my text boxes and sent me back

eventually I made it to the unit manager
where I stayed for a week while she
caught up on backed up work

the unit administrator was embroiled in a crisis
so I remained on her desk for two weeks

my paper was yellowing and stained
when I reached the program manager
who misread my print and sent me
in the wrong direction

after correction I came at last
to the chief operating officer
who left me with her secretary
for another two days

my stay with the chief of staff was brief
only because he had me stuffed in his hands
while he was distracted
he signed me without even reading me

the assistant director passed me on
having forgotten to sign
so I came back again

a couple of months after the beginning
of my sojourn I was graced
by the deputy assistant director
who exclaimed that I was a high alert priority

the deputy director must not have thought so
since I remained there a week

at last I was in the hands
at the top of the tower
I was approved by the director
I was legitimate!

lo and behold
just as I was returned to my worker
ready to perform life saving things

for a youngster whose life hung
delicate on the vine

a new administration took over

all requisitions were now on hold
and under review.

8.11.08

This is what she tells her seminar audience:

As I sat in the lunchroom just after our latest
assembly over our latest act of violence
I scanned the faces and conversation of my colleagues

earnest souls caught in a drone of complaint
about the conditions of their profession
and the pocked clamoring for something more

as I worked to translate their sentiments
into a magic tonic that might hydrate
each of us back into plump vinery
I became aware:

most of my colleagues were consumed
with their jobs and thus without sight
for the children

they were literally not seeing the children

in chills I feared I might have already
caught this contagion

I retreated immediately into a low murmur
of promises

I gave myself an urgent oath
that began with what I cannot do:

I cannot teach them without touching
the dreams they stow away

somehow I must call up something
old and wise within me
and let it touch them

their hearts are bored and lonely land
sorrow soaks the ravines of their cognition

I must touch them in gentle ways
I must locate something new inside myself

some just born butterfly
and loose it to flutter over to
where they tremble

if that delicate thing of wings can land
somewhere near the perimeter
of their safety zone
they might let me in

I cannot trespass
I need to become invited
a neighbor bringing over their favorite dish
not the nosy neighbor all up in their
private business

the neighbor grateful that this child
has moved in next to me
into my classroom
my caseload
my life
my love

I should build a swing
hung from the fattest limb

of my tallest strongest tree
out in my best-groomed yard
before my terrace cleaned and brightened
with baskets of crepe myrtle and iris

I should welcome this child
to swing on the joy-making machine
I have built in my untamed yard

I have to find a way to let him in

my colleagues bash at times
with bricks and stones
on his doors and windows

they form a desperate gathering
of authority circling his assaulted house

calling attention to all his neighbors
that he is a troubled thing
a menacing worrisome thing
and won't he just let us in?

but we won't let *him* in
and letting is where our bonding begins

when we let down our hinge-rusted gate
when we decide we will not abandon him
in our deepest heart
this is when we touch our fate

for when his nervous skin
receives the rippling air
of our door swung open wide

he becomes invited
he now gets to choose:

do I take this hand
and will I bruise?

no
I cannot teach them without
touching them emotionally

I cannot stand across
the cloud crowned canyon
and yell come to me!

what child would step out onto nothingness
without a blatant bridge

I must be the one to harness my soul
to rising sun

vault across the great expanse
to land on his side
of being in this world

I must come to him
risk my heart on him
make a blood oath that we
shall rise and fall together

how can I teach them
and not love them
what paradigm is this?

how can I guide and counsel
having never brought them near
my humanness?

I must introduce him to the story
of how I became me

others often harden
when they should soften

pitter patter
when their best should matter

teeter totter
that's why surrender got her

look away look away
as young girl cries look at me!

not me
I will love them
so I can learn them

learn them
so I can love them

so they can
having been loved
learn

having learned
love.

8.5.08

The last straw came
when I showed up at the staff meeting
with toilet paper sticking
out of the heel of my pumps

a humiliating trailer
on much less than my wedding day

to top it off a corner of my skirt
was hitched up in the back
stuck in the waistband of my hose
revealing my caboose in all its glory

on a day when of course I had worn
my tattered Minnie Mouse panties no less

they were a gift from my niece
who if she had been there in that moment
would have been on the floor howling
and crying with laughter
along with every one of my co-workers
including my supervisor
and her ten-year-old son

who of course just had to choose that day
to get suspended from school

and I'm just warming up

I drove to work that morning with
the gas cap dangling from the side of the car
as I raced to not be late

you see I ran over my daughter's formerly
AWOL pet frog as I backed out
of the garage

I heard the squish just as I turned
on the radio

I thought the squishing sound
was signal static
until I heard the most blood curdling scream
come from my daughter

followed by her hideous death stare
directed at yours truly

we held the impromptu funeral
in the backyard as my daughter
prayed out loud for God to forgive
her "murderous mother"

finally I left for work
applying mascara in the rearview mirror
as I turned the street corner
hit a pothole and stabbed a streak
of black cosmetic across my forehead

at the stoplight I thought I would be safe
to put on some lipstick
that's when the dump truck behind me
blasted its horn to alert me to the green light

I shrieked at the blast
jarring the lipstick up my nose

I now looked just a hair shy of insane

at the staff meeting
once my backside was covered
and the toilet paper removed
and after the laughter died down
into fits and spurts
my supervisor asked me with a face
near bursting whether I had any more
"outcomes" to share with the group

we never did manage to conduct
a serious meeting

before I could crawl under my desk and die
my husband called to inform me that
it was raining and our dearly departed frog
had floated up to the surface in the yard
and could I come home and comfort
our child because she sure was upset
and I was good at those kinds of things

that was the last straw

the next day I told work I was leaving
the planet and would return
when I was human again

I told my husband not to call me
even once if he valued his well-being

I checked into a resort
got a deep tissue massage
then a swedish massage

a hot stone massage
followed by a pedicure   manicure
body wrap   scalp massage   and jacuzzi

I ate strawberries and chocolate in bed
to a series of old romance movies

I listened to Italian operatic promises
and at night cried at the beauty
of the full moon set in a clear blue black sky

I ordered room service when I wanted
soaked myself silly in bubble baths
went on long walks in tall woods

wrote love letters to my closest friends
and joined some children playing stickball
in the street

I picked wild flowers for myself
sang unabashedly with morning birds

when my soul was satisfied
I checked out of the resort
amazed at what it felt like having
taken care of me

I charged this whole affair with myself
to the account we kept for rainy days
the one my husband pilfered from
for his golf habit which paid him in
curses and bogies

I had come to realize that if I am going to
do this work of serving those in need

I had better be willing every once in a while
to go crazy loving myself

lest crazy come and carry me away

in the end beloved frog was laid to rest properly

a stand of sunflowers grew
from that very ground

as for me I've managed to keep my bloomers
under cover and my head above
life's wild waters

I've also learned I can do this work
I just need a little self lovin' sometimes.

8.5.08

She stayed after school

dear child was only 14 when
she came into my office that first day
with eyelids at half mast
her spine bowed as a sapling
beside wind blown sea

as she poured out her story
catching hitching sobbing
I realized we had made her a bag lady
all of us

all over her body she wore the layers
of what we had told her
all her life she was:

at risk delinquent troubled poor
learning disabled oppositional angry
resistant unworthy pitiful
unfortunate special needs
abused neglected abandoned

we had woven a litany of shame
into her frayed composition

she wore each of these labels
as a piece of clothing
piles of burlap and grime
concealing her true nature
stifling her ability to breathe

the ensemble was enormous

in a flash of awareness it came to me
that I could not truly see her
through her stacks of rejection

neither could she see herself
the labels had become her stash
of self-slur and denunciation

she pushed these invectives around
like a grocery cart out in front of her
forming a barrier against the world

she had become skilled at recognizing
put-downs scattered around her home
in the streets   at school

she would pick up that litter
put it in her overburdened cart
make it hers

she was hoarding stained trinkets
from society's gutters
stuffing them into her awful identity
fiercely protecting her putrid pile of self ideas
from anyone who tried to take an item

this dear child had burrowed deep into
the accumulation of our insults
and now was beating us to the punch

she was calling herself these things
before we could spit them at her

I think it hurt less to be splattered
with our judgments if she had already
judged herself with the same un-anointing oil

she was a soaking wet creature
hiding beneath a mound of humiliation

she was hiding from all of us
from everything
most of all from herself

I realized nothing was going to ever change
for her

she would spend the rest of her life
scavenging filth as a bag lady unless
someone helped her put down her load

it had to be me

I would be that one steady ground for her
that one solid place
enduring force
unending belief in her world
of shifting sand and sweeping shadows

I would be that sanctuary of stillness
I would be her leaning tree

at first she lashed out at me
a mother animal protecting her den

I had to go on a quest for new language
a different logic

I had to convince her that what she prized
was in fact her enemy
that what she truly needed
she saw instead as foe

I offended her greatly
and still I endured

I said Honey we are going to work together
to take off all these old clothes
unpack and discard all this trash

we're going to teach you how to reject
the garbage people throw at you
you're going to learn to see beauty again

and most of all I promise you this
I am going to change
I am going to learn a new language for you

my understanding was rising
we her caretakers and authorities
had been persistently waiting for her
larvae state to transform into
a winged attraction

what she needed instead was for us to
look at her with new eyes

to see the butterfly morphing inside her chrysalis
so we could tell her stories of who she was latently

she needed our bridge to her love's affair

the work was difficult
she had no attraction for labels that told of her value
she did not want them in her cart
did not think she could trade them for
useful things on the streets

we took long walks together
so she could learn how to gather goodness

at first she bypassed all manner of beauty
seemed not to even notice the glimmer

she almost salivated at the pollution
swerving toward it like a hound at the rabbit's hole

when we passed by storefront windows
she never looked at her reflection

when I asked her to
she broke down something terrible

she said:
I do not know that stranger
she terrifies me

all this while I worked at changing
I needed to learn to list her good things first

I came up with new names for her
I shared them with my colleagues
friends and family
forcefully

I was determined to plant new seeds

when she struggled with a school exam
I called her a rare and priceless learner

I talked about her anger as a molten fire
that she would smelt into gold

I learned to call her magnificent   majesty
I called her Oshoon

I called her great   glorious   glowing
even if I had to convince myself first

before I had been her bag lady helper
now I was her beauty chaperone

I kept reciting the mantras of her worth
to myself at night   to her at day

she kept inserting old language
the slings and stonings
with which she was comfortable

I kept erasing her obsolete alphabet

one day we stopped before a storefront window
she stared at her reflection
I asked her what she saw

she said:
I see a beautiful stranger
she scares me to death

in that moment I knew change was on the cusp.

8.21.08

Every child deserves to fall in love
with one teacher

every child deserves to have one adult
beyond the walls of home
see her beauty

one person crowned with wisdom
who says to the child
you are special in my eyes

one glorious soul who walks
hand in hand with the young
down their imperfect path
believing in them with every step

one glistening rainbow whose rich colors
reflect its celebration of youthful spirit
tender sensitivities   awesome possibilities

one fantastic waterfall
whose fluid curtain is a security blanket
of joyful painful compassionate tears
cascading into the heart river of that child

one brilliant sunrise who brings hope
and optimism to gray and stony childhood days

one gorgeous sunset whose autumn panorama
reminds the child that he walks
into a fruitful night
walks closer to a tomorrow
of new flame burning bright

every child deserves to fall in love
with one teacher

every teacher deserves to be loved by one child

one surging tide of life's potential
ocean wide   a smile inside
a flame alit against the dark

fed by her teacher seeing her   giving for her
releasing her on a magic carpet ride
toward her life's purpose

a gallant stride past her current days
to her future glory rays

every child deserves to fall in love
with one teacher

who would step before the train
of adult foolishness and sacrifice herself
so the child might ride into his own waterfall
her own sunrise   his own sunset
her own rainbow . . .

a hopeless optimist who chants to herself:
If I can invite the light of
a child dim and grim

If I can quiet the clamor
awaken the spark
shoo the locusts
shush those who doubt
find what is not seen . . .

an optimist who imagines *if I can*
so she does

I know a teacher
who will always be a teacher
and our child-love for her will always reach her
wherever she may be

for a child who loves the teacher
becomes a mighty reacher

and the teacher who loves the child
well . . . God bless that priceless teacher

her love will return to her multiplied
a million fold and thousands will beseech her

for she is a once in a lifetime gift
for the child who desperately
needs her to be what she is:

so much more than a teacher.

5.12.05

Written for my favorite teacher, Roberta Cocking, to honor and
celebrate her legendary love and devotion to our *becoming ones.*

The worker has grown weary
of her co-worker's sourness and bigotry
toward peers   the community   even the young

and yet she cares for him
and so   beneath a maternal oak
on the lawn by the building at noon
she speaks up:

this is not my anger for you
rather a love tree blossoming in winter

the lash I wield grows from my own
dark marsh boiling

in doing this . . . this scolding
mist might rise from agony
become a revelation of self that frees me

and so
you are hard stone turned into itself
a petrified tree root gnarled beyond recognition

Jesus wept and you told him to get over it
he spilled his heart over human sin
you told him to stop being so sensitive
stop loving so much
thank God he did not
he knew he was born for this

Mohammed met Moses   Krishna   Buddha
in the courtyard to protest a stoning

you ridiculed them for caring too much
and for believing they could change the world
fortunately they were deaf to your frequency

Socrates met the Egyptian philosophers
for tea and some sweet bread
you told them to go home
that they thought too much
over-analyzed everything

thankfully they ignored you
had they amputated their intelligence
and retreated from your judgmental scorn
this world would have diminished that day

you are not the way men should be
you are a bee in the way of men

small agitated pestering flier
you mistake flesh for a flower
seeking to feed from dignity
sacrilege should not be your meal

burying your stinger in an enemy
that is in truth your beloved

you confused barren land
sufferer of dreams born in putrid water
come out of that stench at last
dry your wings on licking sun

her taste finds you salted turgidity
but when she is done suffering your foul flavor
world erupts with blemishes
a sign of healing

clouds stop hoarding their water
madmen are listened to just long enough to share
a priceless truth

children squealing because they are not seen
stop

in dank corners they realize light has broken through
an eye comes with it

now they have a chance to be human
what makes them beautiful blazes on their skin
they straighten their spines and walk out into day

because your blindness has been killed
because your knotted heart is blown open
all living things are free to breathe again.

1.9.07

The following is not a factual representation of Diné culture, but a poetic imagination of aspects of this community emerging from conversations between the author and tribal members.

Four thousand seasons ago, in what is now the Arizona desert, a young Diné (Navajo) man sat on a large sandstone boulder. The sun stood at full height. The desert slept. He stood up to speak to several spirits who had come from another time; a time that greets us now. The spirits were thirsty, not for water, but for wisdom. Their own time was barren of such things as what they sought, here, with this young man before them. He rose. He spoke these words:

My people smoke the peace pipe. We have for as long as the sun has risen across our lands and warmed our faces. We come together in a circle because a circle is life's love song to itself. Love flows better that way. We sit because this brings us closer to Mother Earth, close where she can whisper her wisdom into our stubborn ears.

We sit in a circle and smoke the peace pipe, each wanting lip touching that wooden vessel, through which Spirit flows and takes us to the Great Meadow in our mind. We do this thing before a journey, in the face of danger, or when mystery blows into our lives, a gray cloud dancing on our horizon.

In the pipe, we use tobacco that has been blessed. Many times we also use other herbs for their sweet taste or pleasing scent; herbs such as bearberry leaves, spearmint, and red willow bark. We gather, we sit, we smoke. We take spirit flight. We leave here, this chaos place where touchable things are illusion and shadows howl like coyote through the day. We go on spirit wings to the Great Meadow in our mind.

For each of us, this meadow is its own unique beauty. It is a place where the water runs clear, the wind brings good word, the Earth is black and fertile. The trees are plenty; the grass whispers; eagles patrol a deep blue sky. Most of all, in this meadow, we find ourselves; we find our Essence. That Essence has been a wild horse loosed from our hold, untethered and roaming as we stumble through our practical lives. But here, beside the crystal water, where every living thing speaks and we can hear, we find reunion with our Essence. We sit with our Essence after approaching it slowly, careful not to scare it away. For wild things will always seek freedom and this world that men have created is a prison of daunting magnitude.

We sit with our Essence, it calms us immediately. We begin to experience its shimmer as words painting themselves across our consciousness. The portrait is brilliant and expansive, its colors so powerful they combust, become clouds, heavy, swollen, pregnant. Those clouds rain, we stand beneath the shower, become painted in the glory of our own truth. We call this pipe the peace pipe because it is only by traveling on the journey of self-discovery that one may attain peace. Truth is that destination.

My people are teachers. We smoke the pipe also when we prepare for the journey of learning, a journey that binds us to the students, like corn to husk, seed to root, sun to light. You have been told that my people smoke the pipe to bring an end to war. You have been told wrong. What we do, more than anything, does not end war. It prevents it. By visiting our Essence, we are reminded of why we are here. Why we were born teachers. We remember the truth of our nature— that we burn for growth and rage at the dying of the soul.

Our Essence scolds us for forgetting that the sacred bond between teacher and student is formed in the mist of transformation and humility. That to be a true teacher we must become a student *of* the student. That we must invite the student to release her greatness, become her own teacher.

We must fold our ego into silence and stroke the embers of a quiet child soul into a proud symphony of flame. For fire is not so much destructive, as you have been told. It is reconstructive. It takes away the pollution of life and beckons new growth from the soil of a resurrected garden. In teaching we must be willing to bleed, to die of our old selves and become new in every student. They will carry our spirit forward in their living. Their life shall be our offspring. But to truly teach, we must shed old skin. Every moment of every day, we must begin again.

Our elders told us that one day the world would change. That the noise of *civilization* would drown out the sweet, tender song of the human spirit. And in that dark dusk a crisis would be born. Children would die away in great numbers, and in spirit long before in body. Our elders told us that blind men would seek to end this plague by spewing forth more *civilization*—more noise.

The crisis would continue walking toward the Great Death. Our elders told us that there would be one medicine and one medicine alone for this plague: Teachers. Brave souls who would somehow recover the old ways. They would come together, sit in a circle, smoke the peace pipe, find the courage to flee their false selves and sojourn to their own Divine Meadow for a reunion with their truth. Here they would sit beside their Essence and remember the reason for their Love, their passion, their deep ache, their many tears. Here they would summon courage, walk back through the woods to a wanting world . . . and they would teach.

This is what I have been told, by the elders and by my own spirit. More important this day is not what I have been told. More essential is this: What does *your* spirit speak to *you*?

The last words the young Diné spoke were:

May this day hold well my words, for I fear a great dying is soon upon us. Still, I see the sun has risen and is of a proud height at this moment. There is more life to live. My heart beats with a hopeful blood.

8.4.04

She walks with a palsied limp
is taunted as slow for her lisp
and scholastic tracking
loves wearing daisy prints
tells fantastic stories to her pet retriever
yet never utters a word
of these fables to others

except for her mentor
whom she adores

she is a closed music box
playing concertos in private

when the box is pried open
it yawns silently
gives up no song

one afternoon by the lake
she hugs her mentor
with a love song:

walking through life with you
is like holding hands with sunrise daily
you lift me up on thermal ribbons
you sew me with crystal light

I cannot look away from you
disbelief tangos with gratitude
on the dance floor of my heart

you bind my wounds with
the salve of your goodness

you *see me* through my
layered thickets of imperfection

am I an excavation
your inner government grants?

will you unearth all my pottery
the shards of bowls
tiny specks of spoons and ceremony

evidence of my prior diet
the stone toy I played with beneath
the drainage pipe of lonesomeness?

how long do you get to keep digging?
I hope at least until my bones
come up and bleach in blinding waves

use your hands for this meal
your utensils are useless
but how I Love the dewy kindness
of your steep-striated fingertips

dig me deep
excavate what I am into who you are

a sunrise I hold hands with
my superficial burned away
on your sizzling orb
my elated soul aloft
from Earth so gladly.

9.28.07

She has been told terrifying things
about *those people* all her life

now she will be working with them
serving them

she makes a date with her fears
sits down at the table where
prejudice has already been served
and pours the wine of determination

she can be heard mumbling to herself:

truth is
I am afraid of these children

we attribute the horror of their internal poverty
to everything but our own prejudice

we never bite open the rotten seed
it is left to grow to allergen weed
across the careless expanse of fiscal seasons

I need to bleed past the crust of comfort
and fill the vessels that matter so far as peace
shake the shudder   roil   creep of fear

humility is not my familiar yet
ego masquerades as sensitive soul wronged
I scatter wings of flying things
who would approach

heavy-handed batter at the sky
whipped defense with reckless lash
perimeter casualties more apparent
than those close at home

roam the roads   teacher
find the stones   abandoned
reason to stop and kick
what of the progress to be made?

even leathered lizards seek the shade
the need though is for endurance
and sharp will
when sweat brims upon us

trespass first   on soil of soul
then the pain

after this we learn the ways to abbreviate
the shake   shudder   roil of dagger stab
swing   rake   claw   roar
we have it now   the way

child defense barricades itself within
bricks on mortar   limed and grain
stay mortar shells from the breach
august ripening of this as twelve-moons pass
into revolutions numbering more than teens

we come to grown
and seek the stone
to kick and stay us
from the childish ways which gray us
to the colors we could touch

too much pain
too strong the habits
I am afraid
you hurt me so deep
how do I defend but to scream
how do I avoid but to anger
rage is the one thing whose flame
offers me protection from you
who hurt me

now I take control
and hurt myself
and all who trespass upon
or enchant my tethered soul

see this madness?
who can love this way?
tonight I cut the umbilicus
to lies that raised me

this day I blank the slate and raise the query:

what snap will loose the lock?
what force will send flying
this grounded flock?

what light will kiss freedom
into the breast of our humanity?

what nudge to send the boulder rolling?
what to unclench fearful fist of heart?

what light to thaw the frozen soul?
which breath to release the bud?
break open dams?
seduce the grass to dance?

whose first shy step forward
will commence this long romance?

I say mine shall be that step

when she is inebriated
on this reckoning with
a lifelong dysfunction
in her way of seeing others
she leaves the table

and stumbles home smiling

she carries a new heart
free of inhibition
and clean enough to serve.

5.23.99

Who comes to walk among
the meek should not seek
reward in material creek

in that water fool's gold
shall be panned for eternity

those who drink from this
fill mouths with deceitful water
and die of thirst halfway home

seek instead the barley for your bread
in the mindful sight born of a higher state
that recognizes everlasting quiver
of human strands in nature's web

your riches live inside relationship
invest in this and your returns will grow
regardless the fickle swoons of commodity

locate the frequency at which beauty speaks
in the chambers of a dawning life

tune your instrument to this
and you will have more than wealth
you will have become wed to bliss

and spilled your purse
over all who walk with you.

3.12.04

After many nights of sleep disturbed
she is ready

she sits with her colleague
over tea

by the second cup
she finds her courage

she starts:

I know you are a good person
with a caring heart

I know you are intelligent   skilled
experienced after all these years

but you are killing the light
in these young lives

you are killing the joy in your colleagues

your attitude and energy dishonor
the legacy of your years of service

she knows her colleague will react defensively
she does at first

the reaction is a long litany
of merit and worth:

nobody has put more into these youth
than I have

I have sacrificed my health   income
time with my family and more
to do this job

I have put up with the dysfunctions
of this system

endured daily crises and stress

the youth don't appreciate
what I do for them

more and more of them keep
flooding through the door
broken   angry   alone

my caseload grows higher
my resources thinner

I'm not a magician
I'm not a miracle worker

facing this resistance she tries again:

my dear   even your reaction
tells the story of your bitterness

do you not see how your resentment
stings the hearts of the ones
you claim to serve?

you cannot resent them and truly serve them
cannot scorn them and still uplift them

cannot make them trust you
when you have no faith in them

and all the knowledge you possess
is not reaching your co-workers

you have shut the door of your compassion
in their startled faces

they respect your insight and want
to come to you for mentorship

but you drive them away with your vibe
that says don't bother me

the problem is you no longer bother
you do not bother to listen
to learn   to teach   to grow

your emotions have calcified
in your chest

you bring hardened feelings
to the office each day

petrified wood that once was supple
and pliant but now is turned to stone
under the relentless heat and aridity
of your disillusionment

you bring us this rock-wood
to place on our office hearth

expecting us to receive it as kindling
for our morale

you do not notice that its stony nature
puts out the flames and leaves us cold and drafty

then you complain about how you
are treated coldly

you brought the chill that haunts your bones

you have lashed hard plates of armor
onto your shield of self-defense

you have forgotten kindness   warmth   gentleness

you say you are no magician
but you are
you have forgotten your magic chemistry
lost your magic touch

you lost your lust for giving the audience
these children
joy

you say you are no miracle worker
but you are

you have saved lives at the last moment
you have changed the course of despair
into hopefulness countless times

perhaps you have lost the ability
to recognize a miracle where it grows

maybe you have missed the miracles
that live between agony and throes

you've fallen in love with your own misery
and she is far from an unrequited love

she courts you back
takes you on long walks of pessimism
and negativity

when you return you have no appetite for joy

once you carried a sunny disposition
the strains of this work weakened you
and one day you let your sun go down

I believe it still exists
it waits for you to find a reason to raise it
and make sorrow a delighted dawn

I care for you but I am responsible
for these youth

I am asking you to go home and pray this night
for if you still find yourself stabbing children
with indifference and impatience

if you continue slapping colleagues
with rancor and gloom

I pray you will find the courage
and the grace to leave this work

if you cannot stop hurting children
with your judgment and prejudice

if you cannot join the work
at which your teammates toil
and join it with a humble
open heart of ministry

I pray you will summon the responsibility
to leave this work

only certain souls belong in this
great endeavor that swims inside
the fate of lives

the youth we serve are boisterous
but if you find yourself frustrated
at the constant darting about
of the hummingbird

do not blame the hummingbird
it is being what it is

for stillness go and find a tree
and pray no wind kicks up

if you cannot help but grieve this work
please   leave this work

we can never ever cleave this work
from the mores of loving decency

and please believe this work
deserves our excellence most urgently

the most honorable servant finds a way
to become softened as she is wizened
even as those around her harden

she practices compassion as a daily
yoga against people's inflexibilities

please I ask you
go and be with yourself
ask these questions and find your answers

remember we have a special calling
to walk with the wounded
and do no further harm

she does not know if she has spoken
the right words or if those words
have gotten through

she is concerned that she has offended
but relieved she has been most true

they sit the next time for tea
during the first cup redemption pours out:

I want to say that I have come to realize
all you said to me was true

I do not want ill spirit to be my legacy
I really do cherish this service
and care about the lives I touch

I did pray and when I realized the harm
that I have done my hardened heart
broke and died

a new heart was born in me
I feel new and whole again
I will thank you for the remainder
of my life

you have helped me to see myself
I have made a choice
I choose to learn and teach
and heal my wounds

I choose to speak lovingly
to listen with compassion
and to act bravely against the storm

I choose grace and dignity
over stern intimidation

humility over derogation
beauty over ugliness

I choose to act in love
as I serve these youth

I choose all of this because
I choose this work.

9.2.08

She was a principal
and principled

she was a miracle worker
tending to students   parents
staff   administration   media
community   and culture of the day

sometimes losing hair and hospitality
but never losing hope

she was a persistent rebel
determined to love them
even as *power* demanded her allegiance
to convention and not to love

she kneeled down each long day
dug her fingers into the soil
where she caressed them at their root

above ground scarecrows frowned
but all the flowers purred

and the garden
clowned.

9.2.08

He fed his parakeets cracker crumbs
through the bars of their cage
as they pecked at his fingertips
sometimes drawing blood

he thought of his juvenile wards
the *delinquents*

faithfully he kept trying to feed them too
through the bars of their imprisonment

often they drew his blood

he learned quickly that he had to make
a decision about which was stronger
their self-hatred and resistance
or his resilience as a teacher

not a discovery
a decision

he decided to believe more in what
he was born with
than what had been put into them

his purpose over their acquired pollution
his devotion
their absolution

each day he fed his parakeets crumbs
through the bars of their cage

he wondered what it took
for a songbird
once caged
to truly be free

and lose its sharp beak
for drawing blood

one day he brought home a new bird
older and proud
fresh from freedom's plains

the new bird spoke lovingly
with the caged birds
in a common language
known to those born to flight

before too long
the caged birds lost their sharp beaks
grew new down

seems that freedom
is a spirit eternal
alive in the stories
of our true nature
that free birds pass around.

9.2.08

She was going to change careers
until this

she reads the young lady's letter
over yet again:

Dear Mr. President
I've known terror in the cold bed
of my nervous sleep

it crawls through my window
puts frost on my floor

bangs on the pipes
and taps on my door

I've known terror far too well
each day when I wake
fear casts a brand new spell

I know terror in my brother's face
as he slumps off to school
not knowing whether he'll be
shot by a peer or snagged by fate

I know terror in mom's sad eyes
as she serves me half a meal

scared that she can't see half a dollar
coming her way
to pay for the next half a meal
she'll serve to her children
to last a whole 'nother day

I know terror in the hate
that targets my skin
and the dirty desire
that prowls for my curves

I know terror in the chill that spreads
through my nerves as the hopeless
trade gunshots through the night
and I keep waiting for a bullet
to turn out my light

I know terror in the hole in my chest
where everyone's nasty ideas of me
bore through before coming to rest

I know it in not knowing whether
tomorrow I'll be put in the system
or kicked out of school
cause I can't learn

I know it in the way grown folks
shoot disgust through their eyeballs at me
at church as they pray

I know it in our naked school library
with hardly a book

and all the supply money our state budget took

I know it to lurch in the nook
and in the cranny
and in the hospital that turned away granny
cause she had no insurance that day

I know it in my neighborhood's
only insurance plan
the one that says you folks are sure
to get the very last crumb
and if you think we're gonna give
you what the good folks get
you sure must be dumb

Mr. President I know you care a whole lot
about fighting bad guys you call terrorists
say you'll chase them to the ends of Earth

but can you please start in my city first?

I know terror that takes to the shadows
and leaps from my walls

you go to war on terror to keep bad things
from happening but my terror lives
bombs blow up around me every day

bad things
have perfect attendance in my school
make every curfew at my house

Mr. President you go to war overseas
but please
won't you go to war right here for me?

after reading this letter once more
she copies it and mails it to the president
the administration
every single member of congress
and every elected official she can think of

she mails herself the letter twice a year

and she goes out onto the field
to wage love against the cold
that creeps through windows
and leaves frost on the floor.

9.2.08

The young man puts his heart into words
along the margins of his favorite book

the book and the words will now be his gift to her:

Dear Miss
please take good care of yourself

I do not have many beautiful things in my life
I would not want anything to happen to you

please take care of your heart
I can feel you carrying my pain

a heart can only hold so much
make sure you treat yours well
you ask it to do so much feeling

laugh and cry each day
sometimes both bring tears

sometimes neither does
but both break open the scars
that seal our souls to leave them tight and stiff

laughing and crying keep us open
and full of life

make sure to do the things that make you
feel good about yourself as often as you can

learn how to love who you are
make yourself safe on the inside
even if your work doesn't always
make you feel safe on the outside

choose good waterfalls under which to stand

you can't love yourself properly unless
you shower yourself with people who see
your truest beauty flaming as a candle inside

those who love you but cannot see you
are often careless with the way they breathe
in your direction and blow your candle out

forgive yourself as often as you
disappoint yourself so you can be free
to try again with new wings

learn new ways to call yourself beautiful
practice letting hurtful people's words
and actions pass through you
as though you are not there

remember to breathe
turn off your brain when it gets too rowdy

lose yourself in good music
when all around you is awful noise

be an archaeologist
dig for priceless treasures beneath the dirt

shine a light on ignorant conversation
that way you won't trip and stumble
on karma in the dark

fill your mind with your favorite flowers
don't wait for love's bouquet

avoid clouds of human pollution
when you can't breathe your inner air

grow accustomed to spending time
and energy on your state of being

invest in this stock that blesses
its investors miraculously

pay the price for peace

and know
that I pray deeply for your soul
may it dance long and joyful
in its own sunlight
that this world be blessed
by your fullest blossom.

9.2.08

In an early moment of a hiring interview
the interviewer asks the young professional
why do you wish to do this work?

idealism smiles and cheerfully answers:

I just love children and youth
I want to do something to improve their lives

I want to give back and help them
discover their greatness

but will you die for this?

idealism is startled speechless

will you die for this?
what I mean is will you die out of your beliefs
your values   your ways of seeing?

will you die out of comfort   safety   security?
out of expectations   impatience   ego?

will you die into nakedness
vulnerability   humility?

will you die out of control and into surrender?
die out of cultural superiority
and into cultural accommodation?

die out of conformity and popularity
and into a revolutionary's solitude?

die out of socialized identity
and into the Great Nothingness of service?

will you die for this?

long pause and then idealism's response:

how much does this job pay again?

9.2.08

*This one could be called, Bad Spouse, Good Spouse, or, A
Better Way to Butter Your Bread.*

Honey?

yes darling

I can't sleep

what is it?

I'm sorry to wake you but I can't get this
little boy out of my head

what is bothering you?

I'm just worried about where he's headed

he's so angry
his father is absent
his mother detached

he's being academically tracked
because of low test scores
not showing up for school
and violent behavior

he has so much to offer
he is a brilliant artist
but no one encourages him

he carves amazing images
unfortunately he carves them
into his desktop and classmates' lockers

he's wearing the same jeans he wore last year
even though he's three inches taller

I have a bad feeling that he is falling
into an unreachable hole
that he is giving up on life

he's just not getting any love

I'm feeling so limited in helping him
a nervous premonition tugs at my chest

when I leave work
his life is following me to the car

when I turn on the radio his torment
is being played on every channel

when I clear my mind his conflict
keeps clouding my sky

when I come home his deniers
greet me at the door

his bitterness curls my tongue as I eat
his tears soak me as I shower

and now his nightmares have
invaded my dreams

wow darling
he sure has gotten to you

he hasn't gotten to me
his life has gotten to me
we in his life have gotten to me

darling I just think maybe you're taking
too much responsibility on to yourself

his life is not yours to save
he needs to suck it up
turn things around

it's too bad he's not getting any love
but he can't let a lack of love get him down

silence

morning comes

darling I'm leaving for work

okay

what   no goodbye kiss?

suck it up honey
don't let a lack of love get you down!

[alternate outcome]:

wow darling
this boy's situation sure is wearing on you

I can only imagine how being in the middle
of these difficult lives must affect you

especially being so restricted by
policies
liabilities
bureaucracy
politics
norms

I tell you what
let's you and I together take some time
and talk about what we can do together
to help you feel less stressed by your work
and more empowered to make a difference

I want you to pour it all out to me
I want to understand better
the nature of your work

and for right now I want you
to rest peacefully

so know that I love you
I believe in you
and together we're going to figure out
how to change this boy's life

honey thank you so much for that
I feel better already
I love you
goodnight

morning comes

darling please stop undressing me
I need to get to work
what did I do to deserve your
passionate affection this morning?

that? that was for the good loving
you gave me last night.

9.4.08

She wanted to serve *that* community
the one of which we are so afraid

she was conflicted deeply
echoes of her loved ones' advice
and that of strangers boomed
with great industry through
the vulnerable theatre of her skull:

are you sure you want to put yourself at risk?

one person cannot change the world

*why not just put your love into
your own children one day?*

I'm just worried about your safety

what about your retirement?

you won't get rich doing that

your uncle has a "good" job for you

her heart was decomposing cabbage
whenever these thoughts rampaged
her resolve wilted and stank

yet in the absence of this cacophony
her passion rang true
confidence returned

knowing she needed stronger fortitude
she went searching for inspiration

she found it in a manuscript
of desert origins and distant times

it was dulcet to her yearning

it read:

Opportunity lies unseen in the dark
only the illumination of purpose
reveals this cloistered mass

we must project our true self
our genuine destiny
onto that shy plant in the corner
of blackened space

our greatness sits
hot and boiling in the vat
of our disbelief in self

it could rampage through night
and lift the curtain on what may be

but first we must pour

we must pour out our greatness
heave our totality
onto the barely breathing fire

its flames will explode
into pillars of brilliance

the timid plant will catch
both heat and light
become fed

instantaneously
when we cast our Divine reason
for living out across space
we bring opportunity
out of the shadows
and trembling sprout
becomes a giant tree
becomes a forest
becomes entirety

our purposeful life
has always been before us
our vision has failed

we deceived ourselves
into thinking our purpose
was nowhere to be seen

purpose is always before us
like a small child
it aches for our recognition
it cannot believe
we cannot see its grandiosity

it   the canyon of ten thousand miles
we   the ant at its edge treading
in fretful circles wishing to encounter
something beyond mundane

no one owns the manuscript
the container
the map
to the hidden treasure
of our destiny

it is free of human notion
hovers a faithful lover
wed to the one who carries its song

only we can own
our providence
the entitlement is ours exclusively

we bray: *if only I could find my purpose*
to Creation this sounds just like
a horse at river's edge
whining for lack of water

purpose need not be found
we never escape its presence

what we need is a flashlight
a torch of courage
a daringness to project
our greatness across space
to shred the dark into
a billion glints of revelation

to thus behold the timid plant
that in the instance of our seeing
transforms into a towering form

a purposeful life must be lived
before it can become purpose
it must be purposed before it can live

this is no chicken and egg story
this law is so old it has lapped itself
in the currents of time

purpose lives in the waiting soil
of self-discovery
watered only when we dare
to believe that we were born
for a reason   then *leap* toward that reason

can't you hear the music
on the other side of the door?
the party started long ago
you could be inside and drunk
on a fulfilling life

what you bring to the party
sits dormant in a tidy barrel
composed of your rings of fear

you hold all the liquid light
required to reveal your truth

you were born with the power
to erase darkness
and make unseen visible

your barrel needs tilting
then your freedom

but first you have to pour.

2.28.08

He ran into the young lady in the town center
while he was out with his daughters

she ran up to him in a bolt
swallowed him in a hug that broke bones

tears made her face a delta
sun rose from her mouth:

I just have to tell you what you've done
for me

I teach reading and writing to homeless children
in a village in Nepal

all because of a conversation you had with me
when I was a girl

what did I say to you?

I was in a bad place in my life
I had just thrown a fit

you sat down with me
said something that saved my life

you said
I believe all this pain will one day evaporate
and a beautiful soul will remain

you will be fragrance
after the rain

children everywhere who secretly sorrow
will call you a true friend

you said those words to me
I remember each one clear as a crystal

what you did not know was that
just before that conversation
I was on my way to the park
to find somewhere soft and unseen
to lie down

in my pocket I had the pills

I could no longer find anything
to hold onto to keep me in this world
I had resolved to stop looking

that one conversation with you
your gentle magic words
made me want to live

and you know those children I teach?
I tell them this story every time
I feel their surrender come near

that one moment you gave me
and the blessing you placed
inside that one moment
lives on forever across the world from here

in children you have never seen
but have surely touched

I just wanted you to know
your giving made me want to live

he lost all composure
their hug broke all their bones

later his daughters asked him
daddy why were you crying
when that young lady was talking to you?

because my sweet dears
her living made me want to give.

9.4.08

For *all* those who serve children with honor:

They call you *social workers*
but I drink my drinks from *Legend*
so I recall a time
when family and community
were one and the same
it was called a compound

and there were those people
of great sensitivity
entrusted by the adults
ratified by the elders to place their hands
upon the shoulders of children
and turn them to face a better wind

they call you *social workers*
I call you those who turn lives around

you seep into cracks
like salvation blood and fill up the spaces
so precious little ones won't fall through

they call you *social workers*
I call you spirit keepers
denizens of the light
I mean to say you reside
in a house called hope
and keep the light on
so babies and lost folk
can find the way home

they call you *social workers*
but the ground you till is not social
it is spiritual   *of the human spirit*
it drips with black richness like strong coffee
picked from heaven's hills

the seeds you protect are not simply children
not simply tomorrow's daylight
but the reason for our past
and the purpose for our people to be
to be

I drink from *Legend* so I know
mud-caked fishermen work the banks of the Nile
and have a faith that Creation will grace
them with good catch even on stingy days
that they will be able to return home
to their families and fill bellies
with substance beyond yams
this is your name

and the griot
she's old and over by the stump
still got that reach even though her joints are stiff
still got that reach to go on
and pull ripened fruit of symbolism
and legacy from the highest tree branches
and the most introverted clouds

pickin' 'em and pickin' em
and puttin' 'em in her story basket
so that the young ones can fill their
minds with substance beyond what is
extending out to what ought to be
and what used to be

she just griot
and she old
but she young enough to set
young ones free
this . . . is *your* name

they call you social workers
in child welfare

I call you medicine women and men
in family welfare

I call you glue in the community
when rain come to pull things apart

I call you doctors   priests   healers
teachers   palm readers   fortune tellers
prophesiers   negotiators   mediators
advocators   instigators   pacifiers
storytellers   truth dwellers
getting downright dirty
in shameful cellars
cleanin' up mess'
settin' crooked straight

child soul caressers
Man   I call you *masseuse*

irrigators   investigators   neglect haters
keeper of the cage that carries the canary
deep into the dark of human caves
looking for that first sign of something foul
praising that first sign of something beautiful

and then there is this:
in a nation that says this community
is less than that one
and this family is less than that one
and this child is less than that one
and why bother with all that pain
they call you social workers who
go out and keep the faith

only one reason
one reason be
so far as I can see:
even the Blackest   Brownest
poorest   brokest community
is made up of beautiful
families and children
trying to get free

endowed with the full potential of the Universe
unshakable masterpieces of canvass untouched
by foolish nation using the wrong paintbrush

and you . . .
in the morning when you rise
you peel the frustration from your sleepy face
and wash it away down the sink
with all that dirt *System* puts in your way
and you walk clean out the door

cause you believe

you believe these children are good enough
these families are worth enough
these communities deserve enough
and you absolutely have what it takes enough

cause we don't ever make enough
money   material   status   superficial dough
to ever let it be okay to let some folk
not even some kind of folk
slip for just one day

and I ask and I answer:
you have to be warriors
cause you fought my battle
you have to be magicians
cause you carried me over wide water
with your barest feet
you have to be the locksmith
helping somebody who cared
for this little Black boy
silent boy
lost boy

helping that somebody
turn the key and let me just be on my way
to being what I was put here to be

check:
don't you ever think that
any one of these children could never
grow up to become legendary
we are not the wisdom of Creation
we occupy a more humble station
called imperfection
and from this rippled surface
the distorted reflection we are able to catch
is the Beauty of a day on down the path
when the storm calms itself
and quits its crying

warped reflection
in the mirror of child welfare
is the child fared well
is the day's bounty brought home
to somebody's hungry family
to fill bellies with substance
beyond yams

when I began this life
you were there
you carried me
first to a safe way station
then to my people who would
bring me up

child welfare
or child farewell?

I put my money on the honey
the sweet stuff
stories of success
cause I am one
cause you were one for me
triumphant that is
triumphant you were

I am the reason
you get up and go out to work
even in the bitter stretches
when fierce wind blows you back
and sharp sand stings your face

you lean not backward
you lean forward

and I
I can't just thank you
that would be understatement
I have to remind you of your
greatness and how you leave
it in your wake so a child like me
can come 'round and lap it up
and taste some sweetness

it tasted so good to me back then
you want to know why?
because I
I just wanted to be able to grow up
and have the chance to taste
some sweet potato pie

I didn't want to slip through the cracks
I didn't want to erode or fade away
and I didn't want to die
I just wanted to be able to grow up
so I could have the chance to taste some
sweet potato pie
cinnamon in my dreams
fresh from the oven
heavenly steam in my eye

there is something called the system
it is some parts working right
and some parts doing wrong
but then there is the one who toils
for the well-being of the child
made of flesh and spirit
some parts mad revolutionary
calling for change when everything around
seems to just want to sit still

some parts little child on the street corner
selling lemonade
trying to make some coin
so she can get what she wants
to make the day feel good
in her hood

and they
lemme see now
they . . .
call you social worker . . .

I call you Legendary.

I was one of the children . . .

3.28.00

Peace be deeply with you . . . .

INDEX OF FIRST LINES

Jaiya John lives in Silver Spring, Maryland. He is blessed with the beauty of his daughter and serves his life mission through writing, speaking, and mentoring. He is the founder and executive director of Soul Water Rising, a human relations mission stirring the soul to remember itself. Jaiya gives truest thanks to the following:

R. Eric Stone created the cover design for *Legendary* and the Soul Water Rising logo. He is a scenic designer and educator in theatre, and a graphic designer. www.rericstone.com.

Jacqueline V. Richmond and Kent W. Mortensen served as editors for *Legendary*. Arturo Aviña was also a valuable editorial contributor.

Other Books by Jaiya John

To learn more about this and other books by Jaiya John, to order discounted bulk quantities, or to learn about Soul Water Rising's global human relations mission, please visit us at: www.soulwater.org.

*Soul Water Rising chooses not to use endorsement statements in its books.

WWW.SOULWATER.ORG
WWW.JAIYAJOHN.COM